Life

is this all?

a life changing journey of discovery

Richard Broadhurst

Jesus Joy Publishing

First Published and printed in Great Britain in 2020 by
Jesus Joy Publishing.

© Richard Broadhurst, 2020

Scripture Quotations

ISBN 978-1-90797-161-7

Jesus Joy Publishing

a division of Eklegein Ltd

www.jesusjoypublishing.co.uk

15012020

Acknowledgement

Many thanks to my wife, Jean, for her patience over the years whilst this book was being written.

About the Author

As a family man, and a design and chartered engineer, Richard Broadhurst dedicated much of his free time being a youth leader, then a young adults' leader in the churches of which he was a member in his adult years. He was eventually appointed as a church elder.

Richard has been a Christian for over sixty years during which he formed the habit of reading the Bible daily and making notes. His notes included truths learnt from studying the Bible, and material on the Christian life and Faith. With so much life-transforming material, he decided a few years ago, to encapsulate it into a book which could be of benefit to many others. Also, in the early days of bringing this material together, during a worship time, he had a 'picture' in his mind of a text reference to Psalm 138:8; this scripture greatly encouraged him to continue with the book.

His life is living proof of a loving God, and lends credence to the claim that the Christian life is the best life, and has the best ending and eternal destiny.

His previous book, 'Introduction to Life's ANSWER', is also published by Jesus Joy Publishing and is available on their website.

Contents

Introduction

The title describes the book, as it poses a question 'Life – Is this all?' This book sets out on a quest to discover the 'best life', one that contains every provision for this life and beyond. The aim of this book is to show how the Christian Faith can help us to attain this 'best life' through the biblical Scriptures fulfilled and evidenced in people's uplifted lives. A 'best life' for many includes a life that is satisfying and meaningful, which blesses and encourages others, and finishes with a sense of achievement. The method used here to search for this best life is by exploring all the essential elements of the Christian Faith.

Let us first consider a range of lifestyles people are tempted to pursue. People often pursue lifestyles that put a high priority on money, education, power, sexual freedom, ruthless ambition, fame, or even criminal activity, as a way to get the best out of life. But whilst these lifestyles will appeal to many, and may lead to worldly achievement, they fail to provide the best. Whilst many of the driving motivations in these lifestyles are commendable, they lack one essential element - the vibrant, spiritual dynamic in the life of a Christian disciple.

The lifestyle of a Christian, is often misunderstood, or falsely depicted. Whilst Christians, like others, can face tough times, it should be remembered that there is much to commend the Faith as they are the largest Faith group in the world at around 2.2 billion members.[1]

These pages contain all the essential elements of the Christian Faith to help people from a non-Christian background to understand it. For those who have made a Christian commitment, it provides the material and support to aid maturity in the Faith. It uses the Bible as its basis of divine authority and shows the powerful, positive and transforming effect that the living God of the Bible has on the lives of true believers.

To see the number of subjects covered in this book, please refer to the Index.

It should be noted that the book is not intended to be a Bible commentary, but takes the reader on a journey progressively through the essential components of the Faith, and later engages them to respond to the important matters being considered.

The Use of the Book

The book may be used for a number of purposes such as those set out below:

- For those prepared to progress through the book to find the 'best life'. Using a Bible will be of great assistance, but the 'best life' can be found without having one.

- For those who want to understand the main message of the Christian Faith, even if they have little, or no prior knowledge of it.

- For Christians who wish to understand/study the main elements of the Faith, and it's teaching material.

- For those wishing to deepen their knowledge of the Bible and to understand and experience more of God in their lives.

- To act as a reference book for those undertaking private or group Bible study.

- To act as an aid in sermon preparation.

- For those wishing to compare the Christian Faith with other Faiths.

End Notes

1   https://www.worldatlas.com/articles/largest-religions-in-the-world.html (accessed June 19, 2019)

Chapter 1

The Lord Jesus Christ

The quest for the 'best life' begins with establishing the truth concerning the Lord Jesus Christ, who he claimed to be, and how this is borne out by evidence of his life on earth, death, work, and his prophecies of the future kingdom and his return.

Starting the quest

Let us consider that a creator brought life into being, and the creator must be God.

The divinity of Jesus Christ is a core belief of the Christian faith. So, because of this, the whole search begins here with looking at the life, the evidence, the character and provision of the Lord Jesus Christ.

At the start of our inquiry into his life and character, we discover that he is unique in every way - in position, power, holiness, grace, and goodness and in His eternal provision for mankind.

The biblical claim is that He is part of the one and only God, The Triune God Almighty, and that there is no other God. These and other characteristics are given and supported in Chapters 1,2 and the Praise and Worship section of Chapter 4.

Readers will rightly raise the question 'what about the position of gods referred to in other Faiths'? This is best answered by asking people of other Faiths to critically examine their belief system for proof of their God's existence. Some reasonable questions to ask would be:

- does their god communicate with them?

- does their god answer their prayers?

- are there many fulfilled prophecies?

- does their Faith have a history of people's lives being miraculously changed for the better by their god?

Well, the Christian Faith fulfils all the above criteria with a resounding Yes. So, at the start of this quest the readers are encouraged to have an open, but inquiring mind and be prepared to ask themselves searching questions such as those given below:

- In what other 'god', other than the Christian God, do we have such solid proof of in the past, and such evidence for in the present?

- To whom can we compare Him?

- Of what other god, other than the Judeo-Christian God, do we have proof of the following:

... a divine miraculous birth;

... a sinless life;

... one who has had so many prophecies fulfilled about Him;

... one having the power to perform miracles (mostly used to heal people);

... one showing such love and grace for people that he was willing to die for all mankind to make eternal life available;

... a miraculous resurrection;

... a miraculous ascension;

... one who communicates with believers in many ways, including, through answers to prayer, directional words, visions, pictures, gifts of Holy Spirit;

... one who fulfils scriptural promises and changes personal circumstances.

The above statements will be a challenge to people of other Faiths, and no Faith, but they are given to let people see what this living, loving God has to offer, including forgiveness, a new start in life and eternal salvation.

The truth of who Jesus was, was revealed to Simon Peter when he said:

> *"You are the Christ, the Son of the living God." Jesus responded by saying "this was not revealed to you by man, but by my Father in heaven."*
>
> *(Matthew 16:15-17)*

The Incarnation of Christ - His Virgin Birth

This world-changing and miraculous event was foretold by Hebrew prophets hundreds of years before it happened, and they also said where it was to take place – in Bethlehem, a small village in Israel. What makes this even more remarkable is that these prophets lived at very different times.

The prophetic statements they made also gave much detail about the unblemished character He was to have, His compassion for the poor, the hope and salvation He was to offer, and also the rejection and suffering He was to endure. The statements also include many titles that were to encompass His identity including Mighty God, Everlasting Father and Prince of Peace.

These prophetic statements are recorded in the Bible, and some of these Scriptures are given in this book.

The virgin birth of Jesus Christ relates to the fact

that He is part of the Triune Godhead [this will be explained in Chapter 2], and for a period of thirty plus years, He was embodied in human form. A miracle occurred when Christ was conceived through Mary by the Holy Spirit. This fact forms a substantial part and foundation of the Good News and joy of the Gospel that was initiated at that time, and is supported by many Scriptures.[1]

The angel told Mary she had found favour with God and that she would give birth to a son whom she should name Jesus, and that he would be called the Son of the Most High, the Son of God and that His kingdom would never end.

This event was foretold hundreds of years before by Old Testament prophets.[2]

The Purposes of His Coming

These purposes were, and still are, extremely important for all mankind as His coming has brought life, hope, the possibility of forgiveness and eternal life. A fuller description of these purposes is outlined below with the Scriptures that support these statements.

An outline of the purposes is given below: [3]

> ...*To bring us life - life to the full.* (John 10:10)

> ...*To lay down His life for us.* (John 10:14-15)

...To seek and save the lost. (Luke 19:10)

...To save those who believe on Him, and give them eternal life. (Luke 3:16-18)

...To testify to the truth. (John 18:37)

...To destroy the devil's work. (1 John 3:8)

His Advent

Prophesied in the Old Testament - Fulfilled in the New Testament

It was prophesied in Isaiah that *"a virgin will be with child and will give birth to a son, and will call him Immanuel."* (Isaiah 7:14) This scripture was fulfilled by God sending an angel to Mary, a virgin in Israel, saying that she would give birth to a son who was to be called Jesus, the Son of the Most High. (Luke 1:32)

Also, Jesus was foretold as the one who was to come from the line of Jesse (David's line) and it was further prophesied that the Spirit of the Lord would rest on him - *"a Spirit of wisdom, counsel and power".* (Isaiah 11:1-2, 10) It was later predicted that the Gentiles would hope in Him. (Romans 15:12)

Fulfillment

Abraham was told by the Lord to leave his country and go to a land that God would show him, that he would make him into a great nation, and that through Abraham all the people of the earth would be blessed. (Genesis 12:1-3; Acts 3:24-15). Later this prophesied blessing is fulfilled.[4]

The Life of Christ

The Lord Jesus Christ is addressed by over one hundred different names and titles in the Bible due to His multi-faceted character which encompasses His many roles. This supports His wide and absolutely unique position in history because as Creator of all things, He was and is before all things.

When He confined Himself to the limitations of human flesh, in the form of a man, He showed us His humanity and humility. He also demonstrated His deity and His power over death, and yet His willingness to submit to death to pay for the guilt of our sin. He showed such grace toward mankind so that He could make eternal salvation available to us all.

The prophet Isaiah's commissioning by God reveals Jesus' purpose and compassionate heart:

"the LORD has anointed me to preach good news to the poor. He has sent me to bind up the broken-hearted, to proclaim freedom for the captives and release from darkness for

the prisoners."

(Isaiah 61:1-2)

This prophecy was fulfilled by Jesus Christ in Luke 4:17-19.

A human and divine life

The concept of the person of the Lord Jesus Christ being one person, and yet being both human and divine is difficult, and some people have emphasised one side of His nature to the neglect of the other. But it is essential that a balance is struck here as the Scriptures provide clear evidence to support both sides of His nature.

His humanity shows His connection with us and as one who is aware of our failures and frailties, yet He is sinless. Whilst His deity and humanity together provide us with a more tangible view of what God is like. Also, it is through His divine nature that we can receive such gifts as forgiveness, hope, new life and eternal life.

The doctrine of these two natures in one person (Christ) is commonly accepted in the Christian Church, not because it fully understands the mystery, but because the mystery is revealed by the Word of God - the Bible.

His Humanity

He showed great compassion for the poor and those who were sick and healed them, but also had words of warning for the proud and those with hypocritical attitudes. His teaching carried authority because His words were supported by accompanying deeds and also provided hope and an eternal future to those who believed Him.

The humanity of the Lord Jesus Christ is clearly demonstrated in the New Testament and prophesied in the Old Testament with a vast array of human feelings, emotions, reactions, actions, words and thoughts. These range from all the common bodily needs of a human being and being subject to the frailties of tiredness, anger, grief, weeping, being troubled, being tempted, experiencing suffering and knowing pain. He practised the discipline of obeying His Father, and praying to Him as an example to us even though He was in constant connection with God right up until his death. Also, He demonstrated love and compassion for others and experienced joy.

There are a great many Scriptures that refer to the humanity of Christ.[5]

His Deity

Concerning His deity, this was comprehensively demonstrated with miraculous power, discernment and wisdom all tempered with grace. He now sits on a throne interceding for us and will be the final judge of people and nations; He has the authority and power to save people from the penalty of their sins and the grace to grant them eternal salvation. His miraculous birth which contradicted the laws of nature when he was conceived in a virgin by the power of the Holy spirit, was prophetically foretold more than a thousand years before; and finally, He is the creator of all things in heaven and on earth.[6]

Undeserved love

The word 'love' means many different things to people, so it is very important that it is clearly defined, especially as it is such a fundamental human emotion. Love embraces the thoughts and actions that strongly desire the best for the person that is the object of our love, coupled with a strong desire for togetherness of heart, mind and action. When this love is between a man and a woman it ideally results in the commitment of marriage and sexual union. By contrast lust, sometimes confused with love, is a selfish sexual desire of one person who wants to impose their will over another person.

In the English language, there is only one word for love to cover a range of different expressions of affection. However, in the original Greek New

Testament part of the Bible, it is defined by a few different words with different meanings and applications as given below.

The two principal Greek words used in the Bible for love are *'agapao'* and *'phileo'*.

> ... *'Agapao'* is unconditional love - the type of love that is not requiring any response in love or gratitude from us for it to be given. Such is God's love towards the human race.

> ... *'Phileo'* is the love expressed between people in friendship.

Both of these words are used in the passage John 21:15-17, where Jesus speaking to Peter uses *agapao,* however Peter can only reply with *phileo*.

His love was shown to many people in all kinds of need, both physical and spiritual.[7]

God's love is the greatest thing. Without such love His justice would alienate us; His holiness would put us out of His sight; and His power would destroy us. Love is the one hope of sinners, and the greatest desire of our hearts should be to discover God's love for us through personal experience.

God's love is unconditional – we neither deserve it, or do not deserve it. We cannot say: "the Lord will love me because ...", or "the Lord will not love me because ..." [8]

Compassion

Jesus had compassion on people, and this quality of love may be defined as being inwardly moved for another; and also, as being stirred at gut level. Scriptures reveal that,

> *"When He saw the crowds, He had compassion on them, because they were harassed and helpless, like sheep without a shepherd."*
>
> *(Matthew 9:36)*

Grace

The word 'grace' is biblically defined as 'God's unmerited favour'. Because we are sinners in God's eyes, we can only expect condemnation and punishment whatever we do. So, it is truly wonderful that through believing in Jesus as the Son of God, repenting, and putting our faith in him for forgiveness, we can receive forgiveness, eternal salvation, and are seen by him as sinless children of God. In the scriptures Jesus is referred to as being *'full of grace and truth'.* (John 1: 14-17)

God's mercy is when we don't get what we deserve such as death which is the wages of sin; His grace is when we get what we don't deserve – forgiveness, salvation and eternal life.

Paul, who had persevered through much suffering and many difficulties in his Christian life asked God for some relief in his situation and He answered by saying:

> *"My grace is sufficient for you, for my power is made perfect in weakness."*

Paul accepted this response from God and said:

> *"Therefore I will boast all the more gladly about my weaknesses, so that Christ's power may rest on me."*
>
> *(2 Corinthians 12:9)*

It is good to know that in every situation we can find the grace we need through coming to God in prayer when we're in need. For God Himself invites us to[9]:

> *"... approach the throne of grace with confidence, so that we may receive mercy and find grace to help us in our time of need."*
>
> *(Hebrews 4:16)*

His Goodness

This word is described here as meaning the goodness that comes from God with no ulterior motive other than to impart goodness out of a free will and desire to shower this favour on us whether we know, deserve, appreciate or understand it. It is, therefore, profitable for all to understand and rejoice in the fact of God's goodness – His goodwill and kindly feeling towards us. Grace is undeserved love – love that has no limits, however, it can include a disappointment, a seeming failure to an expected fulfilment, where God is taking the 'long term' view of a situation because this will produce 'His Best' result for the person. It differs from goodness in that goodness is experienced only in positive terms.

Suffering and New Life

His Cross

The act of crucifixion, apart from being a very cruel and barbaric form of killing, was also considered a degrading type of death, reserved for those who had committed heinous crimes or opposed the rulers of the day. However, it was plain for all to see that Jesus Christ did not fit either of these categories; hence, His death by this method was totally unjust. It was nevertheless foretold in the O.T. Scriptures.[10] He submitted Himself to this death because He knew this was the only way to procure forgiveness and eternal salvation for mankind. Having paid this price, all that would be left to do is believe in his finished work on the cross. However, it is interesting to note that the crucifixion of Jesus was described hundreds of years before it had been devised as a means of punishment. (Psalm 22:14-18) Thus, God had the event planned to fulfil his purpose of reconciling people to Himself through Christ's death.[11]

The manner of the death of the Lord Jesus Christ, by crucifixion, shows us His amazing humility and condescension especially in view of the fact that He was the Son of God. He had shown that He had taken upon Himself the *"nature of a servant"*; had been obedient to God the Father, and was *"obedient to death"*, and even overlooked the shame of the cross.[12]

The sufferings and death of Christ have produced many benefits for humanity, most notably redemption from the effects of sin and reconciliation with God.

These benefits must be appropriated by committing to following Jesus as Lord and Saviour, and also include being justified by his blood and being saved from God's wrath. (Romans 5:9).

His Resurrection

Before the glorious resurrection, Scripture attests to the fact of his having been buried in the sepulchre of Joseph of Arimathea.[13] The resurrection of the Lord Jesus Christ is an historical fact embraced by Christians. It is a miraculous event that paves the way for Christians to enter heaven. This showed God's power at work, and revealed His love and care for mankind in giving them a hope and an eternal future. The scriptures record that the disciples and many others saw him after his resurrection, encouraging them to put their faith in him, and opening the way for them to be witnesses to this fact and so to give out the message of salvation.

The greatest encouragement must come from the fact that he is *Alive,* which is evident because he speaks to us through his Word, the Bible, and answer our prayers,[14] it shows that He has given us new birth – through laying down His life for us, and by taking up His life again he has given us *"a living hope"* and *"an inheritance"* of eternal life. It should be noted that Christ had authority to lay down his life and to take it up again. This is the ultimate authority of God.[15]

His Ascension - Purpose & Evidence

The fact of the ascension of Christ is well attested to in Scripture and provides an assured future for all those who trust Him for salvation as outlined below. His ascension was hinted at by Christ himself when he said to his disciples, "What if you see the Son of Man ascend to where he was before!", and on other occasions He said "I came from the Father and entered the world; now I am leaving the world and going back to the Father."[16]

The New Testament includes the following evidences:

- Christ died for our sins according to the Scriptures;

- He was buried;

- He was raised on the third day according to the Scriptures;

- He appeared to Peter, and then to the Twelve;

- He appeared to more than five hundred of the followers at the same time, most of whom were still living at the time, though some had died.

- It also says that he appeared to James, all the apostles and then to Paul. Again, the apostle Peter testified to a large crowd.[17]

There are many Scriptures that show that His ascension and return to God the Father was planned from the beginning as part of God's overall plan for the glorification of Jesus Christ the Son of God and the redemption and eternal salvation of those who would believe on Him.[18]

Undeserved Gifts

Justification

For a person to know that they have not only been forgiven for committing serious mistakes in their life, but that they are now considered not to have made those mistakes is in essence the biblical meaning for the one who is 'justified'. It is this amazing situation and life condition enjoyed by whoever believes and trusts in the finished work of Christ on the cross for their sin.

To be pardoned of sin and to receive justification from it are two wonderful gracious gifts from God. One follows the other, pardon is first, and justification is next. Many people have used a phrase to explain the word 'justification' as follows; Justification - *"Just as if I'd never sinned"*.

Christians receive many blessings from justification as outlined below. These points relate to the how of justification rather than the outcomes of it.[19]

- It is not received by observing the law, but through faith in the Lord Jesus Christ.

- It is given freely by his grace through Christ's redemption.

- Jesus Christ died for our sin and was raised to life for our justification.

- Justification has given Christians peace with God.

- Justification has come through Jesus' shed blood, and saves them from God's wrath.

- God's gift of salvation brought justification.

- God's righteous act of justification offers life to all people.

Redemption

Our English word Redemption is transliterated as 'buying back'; 'the obtaining of something by paying a proper price for it; so the redeemed are said to be *"bought unto God"* by the blood of Christ; and to be *"bought"* from among men; and to be "bought" with a price, that is, with the price of Christ's blood.[20] Hence, the church of God is said to be purchased with it:

> *"Keep watch over yourselves and all the flock of which the Holy Spirit has made you overseers. Be shepherds of the church of God, which he bought with his own blood."*
>
> *(See Acts 20:28)*

This situation is like someone may be likened to people having a debt that they could never pay, and hence, having to serve the sentence and undergo the punishment. The good news is that this debt of sin is then paid or 'bought back' through the sacrificial blood of Christ.[21]

Redemptive Love

It was the custom of the times with genealogies to list the male line only, but in the first chapter of Matthew four women are mentioned, Tamar, Rahab, Ruth and Uriah's wife Bathsheba, and two of these are commented on here as we particularly see God's redemptive love and grace at work.

> ... One of these women, whose story unfolds in Ruth 4:18-22. is mentioned even though she was not Jewish. Ruth, a widow, married Boaz, became the great-grandmother of King David, and very remarkably, was included in the lineage that led to the birth of the Lord Jesus Christ.

> ... We note also that Rahab *also not Jewish* the prostitute is included in the lineage of the Lord Jesus Christ, and so again we see God's redemptive love and grace expressed through these stories.

Reconciliation

To reconcile means to restore a friendly relationship after an estrangement. People start from a position of not only being estranged from

God, but He sees us initially as His enemy. We are told that *"While we were still sinners, Christ died for us."* (Romans 5:8-10) This scripture goes on to say how God acted to restore this very broken relationship - *"For if, when we were God's enemies, we were reconciled to him through the death of his Son, how much more, having been reconciled, shall we be saved through his life!"* Added to this good news, we are further told that anyone who is in Christ, is a new creation (2 Corinthians 5:17-19). Then He gives them the ministry of reconciliation. (Ephesians 2:14-16).

Meeting Jesus the King

Many of the images that come to mind when we think of a king is someone who rules harshly and metes out severe punishments on those he disagrees with or who challenge his authority or throne. This view of a king is far removed from the character and actions of 'Jesus the King', because whilst He has absolute authority, He only uses it as a last resort, as shown by His willingness to humble Himself and suffer death on a cross to procure the forgiveness and eternal salvation for all who will truly believe and trust in Him for these things. We need to bear in mind that Jesus is not yet king, because his kingdom has not yet come – one of the reasons why we continue to pray in the Lord's prayer *"thy kingdom come"*. On earth, He was a

Prophet, He now is the High Priest and He will be King in the Millennial reign.

Whilst here on earth He showed compassion for the distressed and the sick and met their needs. Also, He challenged the proud, the wealthy and the actions and hypocrisy of religious people who said one thing but did something different.

At all times He acted with grace and patience and endeavoured to win the hearts of people rather than condemn them. The above statement is just a brief introduction to the wonderful character of Jesus Christ, so please read on to discover more. In the Gospels at the time of Jesus's crucifixion, Pilate referred to Jesus as 'King of the Jews' and these words were written on a plaque affixed to his cross.[22]

His Kingship

There is a prophecy of the birth of the Lord Jesus Christ and His kingly characteristics, and His genealogy, is given in the first chapter of Matthew. However, Matthew 1:1-6 & 15-18, reveals this was not just a lineage of kings, but, of people God had appointed to lead to the miraculous birth, and timing. His Kingship was seen in the way in which He exerted control and authority whilst on earth. However, He was not like an earthly king, as He was not concerned with controlling an earthly country, but a Spiritual Kingdom. He was fully aware of all that was happening around him and He knew what was going to take place, and hence, things were never out of control. There are many examples to illustrate this and a few are given below:

- Just before the crucifixion He told the disciples that they would fall away on account of him and Peter would deny him three times before the cock crows, and this all came true. (Matthew 26:31-35)

- Jesus always knew the type of death He would die, that He would rise from the dead and explained it to his disciples long before it happened. (Matthew 16:21-23)

- Jesus knew all about the 'End Times', except for the date, and told them to his disciples. (Matthew 24:1-51)

Further characteristics of his Divine Kingship are seen in His gracious acts, unlimited love, profound wisdom, sacrificial life, speaking the truth in love, and his authority with healing people and casting out demons. These characteristics show His divinity, far beyond any earthly king.

The Characteristics of His Kingdom

The Kingdom of God does not have earthly boundaries, but spiritual ones, where those inside have a relationship with the King, but those outside it do not. The following Scriptures reveal some of the characteristics and development of the Kingdom Jesus was referring to; In John 18:36 Jesus said *"My kingdom is not of this world"*, so we see that He was not talking about an earthly Kingdom but a Kingdom in the spiritual realm.

During Jesus' ministry He said *"The Kingdom of God is near"* or *"at hand"*. It had not yet come about, but it was near. It was coming soon, and Jesus said *"some who are standing here will not taste death before they see the Kingdom of God come with power"*. Jesus spoke about the Kingdom of God that was coming on earth and sending the gift of the promised Holy Spirit. Again, he tells them they will receive power when the Holy Spirit comes on them. All this was fulfilled soon afterwards on the day of Pentecost, and thus, the spiritual kingdom of God commenced at this time.[23]

Paul went about preaching the kingdom and stated that the Kingdom of God is a matter *"of righteousness, peace and joy in the Holy Spirit"*. He says in Colossians, that believers have been qualified to share in the inheritance of the saints (sanctified ones) in the Kingdom, and have been brought into (translated into or transfer) the Kingdom of God's Son. This is all part of the Good News, the Gospel, *"because it is the power of God for the salvation of everyone who believes"*.[24]

The Scriptures also give a warning that some people will not inherit the Kingdom of God,[25] But Paul writing to the Christians in Colosse says that the Lord *"has rescued us from the dominion of darkness and brought us into the Kingdom of the Son He loves."* (Colossians 1:13-14)

When people adopt His values, live by His standards and obey His commandments, the prayer of Jesus is answered, *"Thy will be done on earth, as it is in heaven"*. Although we all need faith in Christ, we will be called upon to have endurance and perseverance. [26]

His Second Coming

Throughout Bible times there have been miraculous events foretold and recorded, such as the flood, the first coming of Jesus Christ and the return of the Jewish nation to the land of Israel.

There are supernatural events foretold in the Bible which are yet to be fulfilled, and a very significant and world-changing will be the Second Coming of the Lord Jesus Christ to this earth. This event will burst unexpectedly on most people as He comes to take His followers out of this world. This momentous happening has been a positive source of hope and joyful expectation for true believers for nearly two thousand years. He will return triumphantly to this earth for His own people, so whilst it will be a joyful day for them and those believers who had died before them, conversely, it will be an unbelievably bad day for those who have ignored or rejected Him in their lives, because they have only judgement to look forward to. [27]

Events prior to His Return

Please note the following is not intended to suggest an order of events.

In the Bible, there are many references not only to the Return of the Lord Jesus Christ, but also to the conditions and events that will occur prior to His Return. however, the timing and control of these events is in God's hands, and in this time frame we can expect many things to happen such as:

> ... An increase in godlessness, lawlessness and religion that lacks God's power and favour. (2 Timothy 3:1-5)

> ... To most people life will be going on normally. (Luke 17:26-37)

> ...demonic activity coupled with religious practices rejected by God. (1 Timothy 4:1-3)

... There will be a significant time of wars, earthquakes and famines. (Matthew 24:6-8, Mark 13:7-10).

... During these testing times, many Christians will be persecuted and some will abandon the Faith. (Matthew 24:9-13, 1Timothy 4:1).

... The Gospel will have been preached to all nations. (Matthew 24:14 Mark 13:10).

... Many will seek to bring the truth of the Gospel into disrepute. (2 Timothy 3:6-8)

... Many false 'Christs' and spiritual leaders will arise. (Matthew 24:3-5)

The hymn writer accurately captured the situation of the world prior to Christ's return:

Our Lord is now rejected,

And by the world disowned,

By the many still neglected,

And by the few enthroned;

But soon He'll come in glory!

The hour is drawing nigh,

For the crowning day is coming

By - and - By.

'The Crowning Day', Daniel W. Whittle (1840 – 1901)

The Manner of His Return

These are the elements of his return which will affect all people:

- He will come suddenly and unexpectedly to many. (1 Thessalonians 4:15 - 5:3 & Luke 12:39-40)

- Every eye shall see Him. (Revelation 1:7)

- He will return as judge. (Matthew 25:31-46, 2 Corinthians 5:10, 2 Timothy 4:1)

- Christians who are alive at the time of His Return will meet the Lord in the air. Yes, we will meet him personally. (1 Thessalonians 4:17)

- He will expose the motives of peoples' hearts. (1 Corinthians 4:5)

- He will punish those who do not know Him, and those who have not obeyed the Gospel.[28] (2 Thessalonians 1:6-10)

God desires people to enter into eternal life rather than eternal punishment. (2 Peter 3:9)

Eschatology - The doctrine of the 'Last Things'

It is the **End** that makes the **Way** worthwhile. The Christian Faith is one where the believer has the experience of a changed life, for the better, for having a relationship with the living God, Jesus Christ, and this has provided the confidence that the End of life, whenever that comes, will confirm that the Way walked in faith with Christ was worth it. Many Faiths are vague in this area, but in the Christian Faith we have positive assurance and clear promises as shown below by a few of the many Scriptures that relate to this topic[29]:

"For everything that was written in the past
was written to teach us, so that through
endurance and the encouragement of the
Scriptures we might have hope."

(Romans 15:4).

Endnotes

1:   Luke 2:10-11, Luke 1:30-35

2:   Genesis 12:1-3, Isaiah 7:14; 9:6-7, Micah 5:2.

3:   Isaiah 61:1-2, Luke 1:68, Luke 4:18-21, Luke 19:10, 1Timothy 1:15

4:   Psalm 22:17 & Psalm 34:20 as fulfilled in John 19:33; Psalm 22:18 as fulfilled in Matthew 27,35-36 ; and Isaiah 53:7 as fulfilled in Mark 15:4-5

5:   Matthew 1:1-17, Galatians 4:4, Phillippians 2:6-9, 1

Timothy 2:5

6: Scripture Proofs for the Deity of Christ - Psalm 22:1 as confirmed in Mark 15:33-34; Psalm 2:6-12 as confirmed in Hebrews 1:5-8; Isaiah 7:14 as confirmed in Matthew 1:21-23; Isaiah 9:6-7 as confirmed in John 3:16-17; Isaiah 40:3 as confirmed in Mark 1:2-3; Isaiah 53:5-6 as confirmed in 1 Peter 2:24-25]

7: Matthew 9:35-36,15:30-31, 20:32-34; Romans 5:8-9; Ephesians 2:4-5.

8: John 15:9; 1 John 4:19, 1 Corinthians 13:8.

9: Some further effects of God's Grace can be seen in Luke 2:40, Acts 11:23; 13:43; 18:27, Romans 6:14

10: Psalm 22:14-18, Isaiah 53:1-12, Zechariah 12:10 Matthew 16:21 and Luke 24:25-27

11: 2 Corinthians 5:18, Isaiah 53

12: Philippians 2:6-8, Hebrews 12:2-3.

13: Matthew 27:57-60, Mark 15:43, Luke 23:51, John 19:38.]

14: The following Scriptures relate to the statement on resurrection: Psalm 22:16-18, Isaiah 53:1-12, Mark 16:12-14, Acts 1:3; 3:15, 1 Corinthians 15:5-8, and 1 Peter 1:3-4

15: John 10:17-18, Acts 2:25-27; 13:34-37

16: John 6:62 16:28, 20:16-17

17: Acts 1:10-11;2:32, Luke 24:1-8, & 30-31. Also see the passage under the heading ONE and ONLY GOD in Chapter 2.

18: John 14:1-3, Hebrews 1:3; 2; 9-10; 7:24-25.

19: Galatians 2:16, Romans 3:24; 4:25; 5:1; 5:9; 5:16-18.

20: Revelation 5:9, 14:3-4, 1 Corinthians 6:20

21: Ephesians 1:7-8, Titus 2:13-14

22: Matthew 27:37, Luke 23:38, John 19:19-21

23: For the Scriptures related to these statements see Mark 1:14-15, Mark 9;1, Acts 1:1-8, Acts 2

24: For the Scriptures related to these statements see Romans 14:17-18, Colossians 1:12-13, Romans 1:16.

25: 1 Corinthians 6:9-10; 15:50; Galatians 5:21; Ephesians 5

26: Acts 14:22 and Romans 5:3-4, 2 Thessalonians 3:5

27: Thessalonians 4:15-18, 2 Thessalonians 1:8-10

28: Matthew 16:27-28, 1 Corinthians 15:17-20; 22-28, 1 Thessalonians 4:13-18, 2 Thessalonians 2:1-4, Matthew 24:32-46, Mark 8:38, Luke 17:26-30, Hebrews 9:27-28

29: Listed here are a few Scriptural texts that relate to the Return of Christ Joel 2:28-32, Matthew 13:40-43; 24:3-14; 25:31-46, Mark 13:1-37, Philippians 2:8-11, 2 Thessalonians 1:5-10, Revelation 19:6-9

Chapter 2

God's Character

His Unique Moral Attributes

This chapter establishes evidence for the attributes and character of God. The supporting evidence is found in the fact that people's lives are changed for good, not from following a set of rules from outside, but from the inside. This change is due to their interaction with the living God who possesses these qualities.

On our life's journey, it is important to endeavour to understand something of the foundational nature of the attributes of God who claims to be our Creator and the One who has a close interest in our welfare and eternal salvation. So, let us begin this quest by considering the most significant qualities that people are looking for in life - to be loved, valued and accepted, and these qualities are offered to all people through the God of the Bible. So, it is a distinct advantage for people to know this God and to recognise that He is unique, being in possession of the following moral attributes.

Love

His love is unique because it is without measure and pre-conditions as shown in the life of the Lord

Jesus Christ. The love of the Lord Jesus Christ was demonstrated to the full when He died for the sin of all mankind and paid the price of redemption for all who would trust Him out of gratitude for dying for their sin.[1]

The depth of His love was clearly demonstrated in that *"... while we were still sinners, Christ died for us."* (Romans 5:8-9)

In Psalm 25 and Psalm 51, David cries out to God and asks Him not to remember the sins of his youth. He had committed adultery with Bathsheba, the wife of Uriah the Hittite, whom he arranged to be killed in battle after finding out that she was pregnant. He pleaded with God to remember His love towards him. It is important to bear in mind that God does not forget as humans do. 'Remember' is a covenant expression, and means to hold something in the forefront of His mind, namely His covenant promise to bless.

Jesus preached good news, healed all types of diseases and showed compassion. It must be remembered that in the Christian life, we are all 'a work in progress' so whilst it is true that God loves us as we are, it is also clearly evident that He loves us too much to leave us as we are.

Grace –unmerited favour

This describes God's undeserved favour towards all people. He not only pardons undeserving sinners, but also welcomes them into His Kingdom. The word 'sinner' refers to the condition of the whole of mankind who inherently fall short of God's standards and rebel against His benevolent rule over us. In Psalms 86:15 God is seen as compassionate, gracious, abounding in love and faithfulness to David. God's grace also includes His great patience not only to David, but to Moses, Peter and believers today. Ephesians 2:8-9 shows that people are saved through faith in Christ and that it is an undeserved gift from God that cannot be earned; we therefore have no grounds to boast about it since we did not earn it.

Another aspect of God's grace is His compassion. This may be defined as the ability to be moved by another's suffering or weakness. He has the ability to handle all circumstances in people's lives, and this can be seen in compassion as He reaches out to the undeserving, and those in tough situations not of their own making. A wonderful truth has been stated that 'Grace is getting what we don't deserve' which refers to God's forgiveness and redemption; whilst 'Mercy is not getting what we deserve', referring to God's judgement and punishment for our sins.

Mercy

It says in the Scripture that because God has such great love for us, even when we were dead in transgressions, his grace was available to give new life and salvation for he is rich in mercy. (Ephesians 2:4-5). The richness of God's mercy was further shown to Paul even though he was once a blasphemer, a persecutor of the church and a violent man, because he acted in ignorance and unbelief. So, let us remember that as the character of God does not change, this mercy is also offered to us. (1 Timothy 1:12-14, James 2:12-13)

Goodness

God's attitude towards His creation has always been good and His goodness is sustained through all of time because He does not change (Hebrews 13:8), and this is supported by Jesus' statement that, *"A good tree cannot bear bad fruit, and a bad tree cannot bear good fruit."*[2] (Matthew 7:18) Then in New Testament times God sends the Good Shepherd who lays down his life for the sheep. (John 10:11)

His goodness is part of His unchangeable nature, so that all He creates is absolutely good. Sadly, history teaches us that although creation was originally created good, it later became corrupted.

Forgiveness

God's forgiveness has a unique quality in that He does not just forget our sins, but chooses to remember them no more, which means they are gone and will not be held against us in the future.[3] In the New Testament it states that when we confess our sins, He will forgive and purify us, (1 John 1:8-9). Also, it affirms that, *"by one sacrifice he has made perfect forever those who are being made holy."* (Hebrews 10:14)

Reconciliation

Another characteristic of God is that He is patient with us and does not want anyone to perish. Therefore, He waits for us to turn to Him or be restored back to Him (2 Peter 3:9). Psalm 23 states, *"He restores my soul. He guides me in paths of righteousness."*[4] Paul writes *"if anyone is in Christ, he is a new creation; the old has gone, the new has come!"*[5] (2 Corinthians 5:17-19).

Fatherhood

Since there are many young people who either do not know their father, or have had a bad experience of a father, this topic will help to reveal the true character of a father who shows love, care and discipline to prepare his children for a worthwhile life. The Lord wants to be a true Father to all who trust in Him; and so, He shows 'tough love' as well as tender, loving care. His discipline for their good and for the purpose of bringing them to maturity. Proverbs states, *"don't despise the Lord's discipline, because, as a father, he disciplines those he loves."* (Proverbs 3:11-12) Also, when the Israelites were going through the Egyptian desert the Lord carried them as a father carries his son (Deuteronomy 1:30-31). Furthermore, we are told in Corinthians that He will be a Father to those who believe on Him, and they will be His sons and daughters. (2 Corinthians 6:18). Hebrews reassures us that God is calling His children to endure hardship as discipline, like a father treats a true son, because it produces righteousness and peace in them. (Hebrews 12:7-11)

His Truth

Arguments over the truth have always caused contentions and wars, particularly between people of differing Faiths. However, the Bible boldly states that all **TRUTH** is in Jesus Christ who *"created all things in heaven and earth visible and invisible, and ... is before all things; and is head of the church, so that in everything He might have the supremacy."* (Colossians 1:15-18.) The whole substance of **Truth** is **in**, and emanates **from** Jesus Christ. Also, John's gospel states: *"For the law was given through Moses; grace and truth came through Jesus Christ"*.[6] (John 1:17) His truth is absolute, trustworthy and reveals true facts about the conditions and motives of people's hearts, and so provides the standard against which all else can be judged and sound laws based.

One should remember that Jesus said, *"I am the way and the truth and the life ..."*- the way to God, the truth about God, and the life of God. (John14:6) In view of the statements about truth given here, no one should teach as doctrine the precepts, or rules, of men. (Mark 7:6-8)

Truth and love are a couplet that should not be separated because all truth and no love is harsh and off-putting whilst all love and no truth is misleading, and gives a false sense of security. According to Ephesians *"speaking the truth in a loving manner"* (Ephesians 4:15) should be the method adopted.

Purity, Sinlessness and Incorruptibility

These attributes are illustrated in Hebrews 7, where it describes Christ as being a high priest who is holy, blameless and pure, exalted above the heavens. (Hebrews 7:26-27)He sacrificed Himself for the sins of all people (1 Peter 2:22-23) and was a worthy sacrifice in God's eyes because He committed no sin, and no deceit was found in His mouth: Further, John's epistle describes Him as pure. (1 John 3:3)

Holiness

God's holiness is expressed in the fact that He is separated from anything evil and separated to all that is perfectly morally good, and has a nature that is distinct from all his creatures, and is exalted above them. For example, He declares, *"My thoughts and ways are higher than those of man."* (Isaiah 55:1-8) This characteristic of God being holy is a very difficult thing for most people to understand, because of a strong tendency within them to go their own way in life, follow their own thoughts and objectives, sometimes despite warnings, and which results in a life that is not following a high moral code that meets God's requirements. By contrast, God is completely separated from anything that is impure, sinful or evil according to His exclusive high standards and nature.

These who believe in Jesus as the Son of God, are referred to as *"the temple of the living God"*, because God says, He will live with them and walk among them. Also, He urges them to live lives separated to God, and He will be a Father to them.[7] For example, in terms of conduct, it is God's will that you should be sanctified, that you should avoid sexual immorality; *"that each of you should learn to control his own body in a way that is holy and honourable, not in passionate lust like the heathen, who do not know God."8* (1 Thessalonians 4:3-5).

People are seen by God as 'righteous' when their faith is placed in Jesus (Romans 3:22-23).

All people should be overawed by His holiness. Hence, all Christian activities should be carried out with an awareness of God's hatred of sin. People are not likely to be much affected by the doctrines of love and grace unless they are first aware of His holiness.

Believers are asked to prepare their minds for action, to be self-controlled and obedient, and as Apostle Peter enjoined, *"... just as He who called you is holy, so be holy in all you do."* (1 Peter 1:13-16)

Because God alone is holy, we read that:

> *"All nations will come and worship before you"*
> *"Who will not fear you, O Lord, and bring glory to your name? For you alone are holy. All nations will come and worship before you, for your righteous acts have been revealed."*
>
> *(Revelation 15:4)*

Righteousness

This means that He has the character of being right or just, in all His thoughts and acts.

The Psalm shows God's all-encompassing righteousness:

> *"The LORD is righteous in all his ways and loving towards all He has made."* [9]
>
> *(Psalm 145:17)*

Justice

> *"His works are perfect, and all his ways are just - who does no wrong, and who is upright and just."*
>
> *(Deuteronomy 32:3-4)*

This is illustrated in the parable that Jesus told about the unjust judge, who neither feared God nor cared about men. When a widow repeatedly came to him with a plea, he finally met her request for justice. We see that this judge acted justly in the end; so how much greater justice will God bring to his own people. [10]

Judgement

Please note also *"we must all appear before the judgement seat of Christ"* [11] The good news is God will judge men's secrets through Jesus. (Romans 2: 14-16) This is good news for believers because they have received the imputed righteousness of Christ, and will be seen by the Judge as cleansed and forgiven. There are many Scriptures that refer to God's warnings and judgements in the Old and New Testament.[12] It is noteworthy that in John 3:16-18, the word **perish** is used because it is associated with God's Judgement and has great significance, and W.E.Vine defines the word perish in the Greek as, "The idea is not extinction but ruin, loss, not of being, but of well-being".

The Hebrew people were guilty of sin because they had rebelled against the Lord at the Red Sea and they soon forgot their miraculous deliverance from the tyranny of Egypt. This was followed by their wanton craving in the wilderness, and the Lord gave them their request, but sent judgmentally and leanness into their soul. (Psalm 106:6-15)

In Romans 2:4-5, we are warned not to show contempt for the riches of His kindness, tolerance and patience; rather His kindness should lead us towards repentance, because stubbornness and unrepentance will store up God's wrath, when his righteous judgement is finally revealed.

It should always be remembered that God states, *"Every knee will bow before me; every tongue will confess to God."* (Isaiah 45:23) furthermore, *"each of us will give an account of himself to God."* (Romans 14:12)

Whilst there are severe judgements in many Scriptures, including being excluded from God's presence; thrown out into darkness, where there will be weeping and gnashing of teeth. (Matthew 25), let us remember it is God's heart that He is patient and does not want anyone to perish, but for everyone to come to repentance. (1 Timothy 2:4 and 2 Peter 3:9) Also, Jesus is now our Advocate with the Father as well as being High Priest.

The Heavenly Reward – a brief introduction

Let us remember that Jesus preached about Heaven and Hell, so there are important topics for all Christians to seriously consider. This glorious place of Heaven was referred to by Jesus as 'near', and that those who follow Him will receive great rewards in Heaven. (Matthew 5) Christian followers are required to *"set [their] minds on things above, not on earthly things".* (Colossians 3:1-2) So that whilst on earth the underlying desire of the Christian is to live to please Him and fulfil His will. So whether on earth or in heaven, all who have a relationship with Him will be with Him. Jesus encouraged us to *"rejoice that your names are written in heaven"* (Luke 10:20). It is also promised of believers that their *"… names are in the book of life"* (Philippians 4:3)

There is a place He has *"prepared for us"*, and will *"come back for us"* (John 14:3), because He wants us there (John 17:24), and there are the encouraging words:

> *"No eye has seen, no ear has heard, no mind has conceived what God has prepared for those who love him."*
>
> *(1 Corinthians 2:9)*

Hence, every person should give careful consideration to the Scriptures in Matthew 24:15-22, Luke 10:20, Philippians 4:3 to assess whether their names are *"written in heaven"* also referred to as *"the book of life"*.

Those to be found in heaven will be those who have believed in the Lord Jesus Christ as God's Son and Saviour (John 3:16-18 John 3:36), having acknowledged and confessed their sin.[13]

The Ultimate Judgement of Hell – a brief introduction

The subject of Hell is not often taught in churches because it is much more acceptable to teach about love, but both should be preached to present a balanced gospel message, as this would be following the example of Jesus who preached about both subjects.

To help understand this topic, God's view of sin must be taken into account as from the beginning he decreed that the serious nature of sin had to be punished, and the only one who could pay the price for the sin for all mankind was the sinless Son of God, the Lord Jesus Christ, and He paid the ultimate price for all people on the cross.

The root meaning of sin is 'missing the mark' or 'falling short of a goal', as it says:

"... for all have sinned and fallen short of the glory of God"

(Romans 3:23)

In his epistle John says *"sin is lawlessness"*. (1 John 3:4) Basically, living life for ourselves by doing what we want to do without reference to God, and ignoring or rejecting God's sacrificial death for us, is **sin**. It explains in Hebrews that "without the shedding of blood there is no forgiveness." (Hebrews 9:22)

It follows, therefore, that for those who reject or fail to receive Him and His loving gift of forgiveness, stand condemned. As it says in John gospel:

"... whoever does not believe stands condemned already because he has not believed in the name of God's one and only Son."

(John 3:18)

This rejection results in people being left to pay their own price for sin which is the suffering of Hell also called the Lake of Fire or Ghenna, that is described by Jesus in shocking terms in various Scriptures.[14]

However, it is not God's heart that we should pay the punishment for sin. This is because He has paid the penalty for all who repent and believe on Him, as made clear in 1 Timothy 2:3-4.

Jesus gives further warnings when He warned us to, *"be afraid of the One who can destroy both soul and body in hell."* (Matthew 10:28) Also, He warned about those who caused children believers to sin, and how this would bring them into judgement. (Mark 9:42-43)

Also, there are warnings in Scripture that preachers should preach the whole gospel.[15]

Claims made by Jesus Christ

Jesus makes a number of unique claims as "I am..." in absolute terms, as shown below:

- *"I am the bread of life"* – John 8:28, John 8:12, John 8:28, John 8:58, John 10:9

- *"I am the light of the world"* John 8:12

- "When you have lifted up the Son of Man, *then you will know that I am the one I claim to be ..."* John 8:28 He is claiming that people will only understand what He was to achieve through His death, resurrection and life thereby offering us eternal salvation

• *"Before Abraham was, I am"* John 8:58

• *"I am the gate; whoever enters through me will be saved"* John 10:9

• *"I am the good shepherd. The good shepherd lays down his life for the sheep."* John 10:11

• *"I and the Father are one."* John 10:30

• *"I am the resurrection and the life."* John 11:25

• *"I am the way and the truth and the life"* John 14:6

• *"I am the true vine, and my Father is the gardener".* John 15:1

Other Attributes

Surely what most people are looking for in life is to have the security of living in the warmth and protection of a loving Father figure, a Supreme Being, who is all knowing so cannot be deceived and whose true justice and judgement is never blurred or compromised. Also, someone whose power to act with perfect wisdom is never found wanting, and whose supernatural creative and healing power has been demonstrated over all time. Well, it is this Supreme Being whose attributes we are further considering.

So, to complete the overview of the attributes of God, it is necessary to consider His other attributes. He is a mighty, majestic, perfect and immense God who is all-knowing, all-seeing, all-wise. Not only is He the creator of all, but is the **One** who always shows such love and consideration for the relative frailty of His creation which includes human beings, bearing in mind that He sees the 'big picture' and knows the beginning and the end of all people and events. He also knows of the problems that are caused by man and those that He allows according to His compassion, wisdom, foreknowledge and purposes.

To enable the reader to discover more of the true nature of God, these attributes are more fully reviewed under the headings below.

His Infinity, Eternity and Uniqueness

These above qualities apply in absolute and exclusive terms to God as revealed in the Bible.

He is not confined to the limits of time and space. His existence is from eternity past to eternity future.

The Scripture states that God will endure for ever and will call the past to account (Ecclesiastes 3:14 – 15).

Also, in describing God it states that he is "eternal, immortal, invisible, the only God".[16] (1 Timothy 1:7)

His Self-Existence, Immortality and Omnipresence (Presence Everywhere)

These claims mean that God, as revealed in the Bible, has no beginning, no end, and is present everywhere at the same time. Also, He is not bound by space and time. In the Jewish faith God is called Jehovah which means 'self-existing One', the One who has created everything, and his name is given in Psalms 83:18, Isaiah 12:2 in the KJV Bible.

The psalmist declares *"from everlasting to everlasting you are God"*. (Psalm 90:2)

In the Scripture referring to the Lord Jesus Christ, it states: *"He is before all things, and in him all things hold together". (Colossians 1:17)*

God is a Spirit

The psalmist asks questions concerning God's Spirit saying 'Where can I go from your Spirit? Where can I flee from your presence'? (Psalm 139) And wherever we go He is there.

In referring to believers Paul states:

> *"You, however, are controlled not by the sinful nature but by the Spirit, if the Spirit of God lives in you. And if anyone does not have the Spirit of Christ, he does not belong to Christ."*

(Romans 8:9)

His Wisdom and Omniscience (All Knowing)

God's wisdom is infinite and He is the fount of all knowledge and hence, knows everything – past, present and future, and no seemingly new thought or invention is new to God.

In Exodus 3:19-20, it states that after all the wonders that God will perform among the Egyptians that Pharaoh will let the Hebrew people go from Egypt. In another Scripture it states *"The LORD is the everlasting God, the Creator of the ends of the earth. He will not grow tired or weary, and his understanding no-one can fathom"*. (Isaiah 40:28).

His Sovereignty and Omnipotence (All Powerful)

With God nothing is impossible, and the only constraint on His actions is that which He puts on Himself out of love, grace and timing to fulfil His purposes.

The first verse of the Bible declares *"In the*

beginning God created the heavens and the earth."

With reference to the Lord Jesus Christ it states that:

> *"He is the image of the invisible God, the firstborn over all creation. For by Him all things were created: things in heaven and on earth, visible and invisible, whether thrones or powers or rulers or authorities; all things were created by Him and for Him."*
>
> *(Colossians 1:15-17)*

It also says that He is before all things and that He holds all things together. So, these statements uniquely describe the Lord Jesus Christ as God.

This name for God is used in many places in Scripture that indicate that He is always 'Enough' and has more than 'enough' in the sense of grace for any human condition, provision for every circumstance, and wisdom and power for any situation in time or eternity.

In these days, we live in a culture that no longer takes seriously the idea of a weighty God but rather celebrates a God who cooperates with our agenda - and that is a misleading statement.

His Perfection and Immutability (Unchangeable)

God's character is one of absolute perfection and this is linked to the fact that He is unchangeable in nature and purpose. He has no need to change because He is, and always was, perfect. Scripture affirms that *"Jesus Christ does not change, and is the same forever."* (Hebrews 13:8). Moreover:

> *"The LORD foils the plans of the nations; He thwarts the purposes of the peoples. But the plans of the LORD stand firm for ever, the purposes of His heart through all generations."*
>
> *(Psalm 33:10 - 11)*

His Immensity (Immeasurable)

The span He covers is limitless and reaches beyond every corner of the vast, immeasurable universe. In Hebrew 'God Almighty' is written as **'EL SHADDAI'** meaning 'the God of the mountains', or alternatively translated 'God the enough' - enough for all powers, circumstances or situations.

Jeremiah records His words:

> *"'Can anyone hide in secret places so that I cannot see him?' declares the LORD. 'Do not I fill heaven and earth?' declares the LORD."*[17]
>
> *(Jeremiah 23:24)*

The Unity of the Godhead - The Trinity

In the Scriptures, we see all three Persons of the Godhead referred to and identified as God the Father, God the Son and God the Holy Spirit. We also see many Scriptures that show their unified and close relationship. Although there remains a mystery about this whole concept of a triune Godhead, it is reassuring to know that there is much evidence given in the Scriptures to support it.[18]

When Jesus gives the Great Commission's baptismal instruction that, *"... baptising them in the name of the Father, the Son, and the Holy Spirit."* (Matthew 28:19), the whole Trinity is included.

An illustration of 'The Trinity

If we consider the substance of water, we know that it can exist in three forms: as a solid (ice); as a liquid; and as a vapour (steam). However, all three forms are in fact one substance. In a simple way, the analogy of water can be compared with 'The Godhead' - that is one divine 'substance' that exists in the three Persons of the Father, the Son and the Holy Spirit, - and these three Persons are referred to as 'The Trinity'.[19]

His absolute supernatural creative and healing power

Although God has such absolute power it is mostly used in a positive, creative way for the benefit of mankind, and yet sometimes it is used in a destructive way as a warning. Nevertheless, throughout the Scriptures we see that it is God's heart to want to forgive, restore and empower erring people:

> *"So God created man in his own image, in the image of God he created him; male and female he created them."*
>
> *(Genesis 1:27)*

He created all the plants, trees, animals and birds. (Genesis 1:29-31)

God's creative powers are given in many Scriptures, including, being creator of the world and universe (Genesis 1:1-3) with all its wonderful and unique features including controlling the Flood and the position and effect of the moon.[20]

God is referred to as everlasting and the Creator of the ends of the earth. (Isaiah 40:28)

Also, in a prophetic statement it says He will be referred to as *"Wonderful Counsellor, Mighty God, Everlasting Father, Prince of Peace."* (Isaiah 9:6) indicating that he will create the peace which is missing from the world.

In the Scriptures we have ample evidence of God's unlimited power and this is demonstrated by the magnificence of His creative, healing and restorative abilities, including physical healing, demonic deliverance, spiritual conversion and regeneration.

Many of the words commonly used for healing are given the meaning of 'being made whole'. In the ministry of the Lord Jesus Christ, sick people were 'made whole'. He had a wider concern than just physical healing, and this included the person's emotional, mental and spiritual health.

He is referred to as *"King eternal, immortal, invisible, the only God."* (1 Timothy 1:17)

In contrast to His high station, He was also involved with needy people, and it is to be noted that He did not impose His will on them but asked them what they wanted from Him.[21]

Endnotes

1: John 3:16-18; 14:21; 15:13, Romans 2:4; 5:8; 8:37-39

2: Genesis 1:31, Psalm 31:19, Psalm7:13, and Luke 18:19

3: 2 Chronicles 7:14, Psalms 103:2-4, Isaiah 43:25

4: Psalm 147:3 and Isaiah 53:5

5:    See John 10:10, Romans 5:9-11, Hebrews 8:10-12

6:    See Proverbs 30:5, John 14:61, James 1:17-18

7:    2 Corinthians 6:16-18, 1Corinthians 1:30, 2 Thessalonians 2:13-14

8:    1 Peter 1:15-16

9:    Ezra 9:15, Isaiah 16, Romans 3:21-22; 1 Peter 3:18

10:   Luke 18:1-8, 2 Thessalonians 1:5-7, 1 John 1:9

11:   Romans 14:10-13, 2 Corinthians 5:10-11, Hebrews 9:27-28

12:   Psalms 9:8; 89:14, Isaiah 2:4; 33:2213 Matthew 10;32-33; 12:41; John 5:26-30; Romans 1:18-32; John 3:16-1

13:   Romans 3:23; 6:23, 1John 1:9

14:   Matthew 5:22-30; 10:28; 23:29-36, Mark 9:42-44, Luke 12:4-5; 16:19-26, 2 Thessalonians 1:5-9, 2 Peter 2:4-9

15:   Ezekiel 3:17-19; 33:1-7, Romans 15:18-19, 1 Corinthians 9:16, Galatians 1:10, 1Thessalonians 2:4

16:   Isaiah 9:6; 43:10; 44:6-8, Hebrews 1:10-12

17:   1Kg 8:27-28, Psalms 8:3-4; 145:3, Isaiah 40:28; 66:1, Ephesians 4:10

18:   Isaiah 43:10-11; 44:6-8; 46:9, Romans 3;30, Ephesians 4;6, 1 Timothy 2

19:   Isaiah 42:1, Joel 2:28-29, John 10:29-30; 15:26, 1 Peter 1:1-2

20:   Genesis 1, Psalms 104:1-19, Isaiah 40:25-28

21:   Mark 10:46-52, John 5:5-9]

Chapter 3

God's Provision for every believer

As the Christian life is impossible without God's help, described here are the resources and support made available from the living Word of God, the Bible. Christ's Church and the Holy Spirit's power and influence further enable the seeker to access the 'best life'.

The Bible - The book with all life's answers

As we reflect on the issues raised in this book, let us consider the provision for life that is given in this Section. Its content clearly shows that Christians are not left without the resources, especially the Person and presence of the Holy Spirit to guide and empower them to live this new life through all its many phases, including the highs and lows. At the end, we will know the joy of being with the One God who loves us, and this is shown by the wide range of resources and help He has provided here for us on earth.

The Bible is acclaimed as the world's bestseller, a book considered to be in such great demand that the full Bible has been translated into over 600 languages, and the New Testament into more than 1400 languages. It can also be said that the Bible is the most enlightening, but dangerous, book in the world because it holds the keys to quality of life, eternal life, heaven and hell.

The Bible, in fact, is a collection of books written over the course of more than 1,400 years, and is divided into two sections, namely - The Old and New Testaments.

It contains a wide amount of subject matter written by a variety of people, specifically chosen and anointed by God, including prophets who received their messages from God; leaders of the Israelites; Jesus' apostles; church leaders. Whilst having many writers it has unique interconnectivity and an unassailable authority due to its many fulfilled prophecies.

The prophetic passages of Scripture contain many prophecies that have been fulfilled and some which await fulfilment. These fulfilled prophecies further establish the Bible's God inspired authenticity, and all the words of Scripture among believers are referred to as God's Word. The Bible is not just a book of ordinary words, but it contains God's anointed and empowered words that have worked, and are still working in people's hearts to change lives, motives and destinies today and provide hope, purpose and eternal life. So, it is important to read the Bible, believe and follow its message to gain what God has to offer through it.

Introduction to the Bible

Many religious Faiths refer to their 'Scriptures' which they trust implicitly, but a reader of the Bible will soon discover it is very different to other Scriptures for a number of reasons. To begin with, the way in which it was written was an amazing and miraculous story. This is because it had approximately forty writers and they covered a 1500 to 1600-year span of time, and yet unknowingly their writings would, hundreds of years later, be placed side by side and made into a book with one story having a vast interlocking unity and cohesion.

This Bible, is not only for priests and people with special training to read but for anyone to read. Another special feature about the book the reader will discover, is that it has a power to speak directly to them, which derives from the fact that it radiates divine authority.

The reason for the ability of the biblical scriptures to speak to people is due to the activity of the living God, and the evidence for this is given in Hebrews:

"For the word of God is living and active. Sharper than any double-edged sword, it penetrates even to dividing soul and spirit, joints and marrow; it judges the thoughts

and attitudes of the heart."

So, whilst God's word can, and often does, make people feel uncomfortable, guilty, and hurt, His intention, through conviction, is to bring restoration, hope and healing. This word also brings encouragement, confirmation and guidance with assured promises.

The Bible states that: *"the word of our God stands for ever"*, and *"My word will never pass away"* [1]

Paul says in that the Word of God is to be used for:

"All Scripture is God-breathed and is useful for teaching, rebuking, correcting and training in righteousness, so that the man of God may be thoroughly equipped for every good work."

(2 Timothy 3:16-17)

One of the many unique features of the Bible is that it contains prophecy and also that warnings are given in Bible that people should only preach or teach the gospel given by Christ, and ignoring or disobeying brings punishment.[2]

Prophecy

Prophecy is a unique feature of the Bible, because it contains a great many statements foretelling future events, and a large number of these have already been fulfilled, further supporting its authenticity as the Word of God.

Biblical prophecies are revealed to show divine future statements given through God's people in the Old Testament, the New Testament and the Lord Jesus Christ. The prophetic statements given in Matthew 24 are challenging, and call for believers to be faithful and trusting in God through difficult times.

In the Old Testament prophecy was particularly related to the Israelites, and the prophecies were given to remind them of their heritage and calling to faithfully follow God's ordained laws. Prophecies encompassed promises, warnings and miraculous events to give both comforting and blunt encouragements for the people to remain faithful to God. There are a number of prophecies that point to the coming of the Messiah (Isaiah 9, and 53), the way He was to come, His character, life and death.[3]

Most of these prophecies were fulfilled, and those that are still awaiting fulfilment are pointing to future events and the end times concerning the Hebrew people and other nations. There are prophetic scriptures in most of the books in the Old Testament.

In the New Testament prophecy is extended

beyond the people of Israel to all people with words of promise and warning and assisted at times with miraculous events. The Old Testament prophecies of the coming of the Messiah, the Lord Jesus Christ, were fulfilled in Matthew 1-2, and Luke 1-2, with a number of miraculous events concerning His birth; life of gracious love; powerful healing and deliverance ministry including restoring people to life; and finally His sacrificial death; resurrection and ascension; thus establishing His deity as The Son of God, hence, providing the only positive proof of God in the world as established by these events and fulfilled prophecies.

Prophetic scriptures are found in most of the books of the New Testament, and apart from those mentioned above, there are many that point to future events including The Tribulation and Judgment (Matthew 10:11-20, Matthew 24:9-14, Revelation 7:14), The Antichrist (1 John 2:18-23), The Second Coming of Christ (John 14:3, 1 Thessalonians 4:13-5:11); The Millennium and The New Heaven and New Earth (Revelation 20:1-4); Signs of the End of the Age (Matthew 24).

The New Testament also contains many Scriptures that refer to God's judgement.[4]

Historical Outline of the Bible

The following outline of the Bible has been compiled from statements by biblical scholars that relate to this topic.

The Bible derives its authority neither from ecclesiastical statements nor from any human authority. The Bible is said to be self-authenticating, radiating its divine authority itself, and it is by the inward testimony of the Holy Spirit that a person perceives, and accepts as truth.

When the Books that make up the Bible were considered to be the very 'Word of God' they were referred to as the 'Canon of Scripture'. The term 'Canon' is used to denote a list of books which the church acknowledges as inspired and authoritative Scripture, established as a standard for faith and practice. Hence, we have the Canon of the Old Testament comprising 39 Books, and the Canon of the New Testament with 27 Books.

The Books of the O. T. like those of the N.T. were inspired, 'God breathed'. But the Holy Spirit worked also in the hearts of God's people so that they came to accept these Books as the Word of God and submitted to their divine authority. The church councils did not give the Books their divine authority, but simply recognised that they had it inherently.

It is considered that when the N.T. Books were coming into being the O.T. Books existed as a completed collection to which divine authority was already given.

In the N.T. the O.T. is repeatedly referred to as *'the Scriptures'* (Matthew 26:54, John 5:39, Acts 17:2), indicating that the O.T. was a well-known collection of writings, forming a unity.

The unity of the O.T. with the N.T. is authenticated by the vast amount of cross-referencing that occurs between them.

In the N.T. we find the Lord Jesus Christ referring to the O.T. Scriptures and also acknowledging that His coming, birth, life and death were all foretold in them and that He would fulfil all the Scriptures that pertained to Him.

The apostolic church was not without Scripture, and looked for its doctrine to the O.T. As the apostles died their disciples upheld the apostolic doctrines and used their writings, and in the 4th century AD we see the fixation of the N.T. Canon within the limits to which we are accustomed today.

The Protestant English Bible

The Protestant English Bible has a long and interesting history, but the purpose here is to give an outline of its main points.

- 405 - Jerome completed his translation of the Bible text into Latin, called the This was of no use to the general population of Saxon people living here, where only the educated clergy could read it.

- 735 - Bede of Jarrow translated the Gospel of John into the Saxon language.

- 10th century - Aldred translated the Gospels into Anglo-Saxon.

- 1382 - John Wycliffe, Master of Balliol College Oxford, resigned his 'mastership', and with others, translated the Bible into English.

  He was determined that the common man should be able to read it in his own tongue. The problem with this version of the Bible was that it was a translation of a translation.

- 1526 - William Tyndale made a direct translation which from the original Hebrew and Greek into English which was then printed so that people could read it for themselves.

However, he met great opposition from the authorities in England, so he went to Hamburg in Germany. To avoid detection whilst doing this secret work meant he had to move from place to place, but after printing, copies were secretly shipped to England. When discovered, many were burnt by the orders of the ecclesiastical authorities.

- 1534 - Tyndale brought out a revised edition and also translated the first five books of the Bible, and the book of Jonah,

- 1535 – Tyndale was imprisoned in Vilvorde where he was strangled and burnt at the stake.

  The success of Tyndale's English translation of the New Testament can be judged by the fact that nine-tenths of the Authorised Version of the New Testament is as he wrote it.

- 1543 - The sale of English Bibles was banned, and there was the persecution of those with these Bibles under Queen Mary.

  Despite all these difficulties Bibles continued to be published to the present day:

- 1537 The Matthew Bible by John Rogers? (Thomas Matthew).

From the above outline of the story of the Bible we can see the time, effort and great price, which has been paid to bring us the Bible in our own language, let us value it, use it and live by it, as it is the Word of God to us.

Important Observations

The Bible

One of the author's main aims for writing this book 'Life – Is this all?' was to help the readers discover the 'best life' they can have, and to show that this quest is fully met in the Bible, not the place people are likely to look. Most people would consider it irrelevant to modern day life, and of little interest. Indeed, people of other Faiths sometimes oppose it and forbid their followers to read it. Yet, it contains a message of hope for life and the future for every age, and every person whatever their condition or situation. Also, its message contains challenges and warnings, and claims to be the only Word of God.

The writers of the Psalms had many positive things to say about God's Word, as evident from the following scriptures:

"Blessed is the one who does not walk in

step with the wicked or stand in the way
that sinners take   or sit in the company of
mockers, but whose delight is in the law of
the Lord, and who meditates on his law day
and night."

(Psalms 1:1-2)

"The law of the Lord is perfect, refreshing
the soul. The statutes of the Lord are
trustworthy, making wise the simple."

(Psalms 19:7)

"All his laws are before me; I have not turned
away from his decrees. I have been
blameless before him and have kept myself
from sin".

(Psalms 18:22-23)

"I will praise you with an upright heart as I
learn your righteous laws. I will obey your
decrees; do not utterly forsake me. How can
a young man keep his way pure? By living
according to your word. I seek you with all
my heart; do not let me stray from your
commands. I have hidden your word in my
heart that I might not sin against you."

(Psalm 119:7-11)

"Open my eyes that I may see wonderful
things in your law."

(Psalm 119:18)

"The unfolding of your words gives light; it gives understanding to the simple."

(Psalm 119:130)

The O.T. prophets like Isaiah and Amos received, recorded and spoke out God's Word.[6]

The actual words God spoke are flawless and should not be added to, or subtracted from, see Deuteronomy 4:2, Proverbs 30:5-6, Revelation 22:18-19. It says it is 'God-breathed', living and active, 2 Timothy 3:16, Hebrews 4:12 and Matthew 24:35, 1 Peter 1:23-25.

The words recorded by God's prophets were not theirs but were given to them by God's Holy Spirit and carried His authority. (2 Peter 1:19-21)

We need to listen to God's Word and obey it. (James 1:21-22) The words make a unique claim as they are: active, sharper than any double- edged sword, they penetrate to divide soul and spirit and judges the thoughts and attitudes of the heart. (Hebrews 4:12)

In the Scriptures Romans 12:1-2, 2 Corinthians 3:18, the word 'transform' refers to changing into another life form, a continuous process of inward change in the person effected by God's Holy Spirit.

The study of the Bible without acting on what it says produces pride and judgemental attitudes. (James 1:22-25)

So, let the reader bear in mind the words of Jesus - *"Heaven and earth shall pass away, but my words shall not pass a way."* (Matthew 24:35)

The purpose of the book of Proverbs is to put godliness into working clothes as it addresses our lifestyle at home, in business and society. The Proverbs provide practical wisdom for all aspects of life, and wisdom for making decisions. An illustration of such wisdom is found in Matthew:

"Therefore everyone who hears these words of mine and puts them into practice is like a wise man who built his house on the rock. The rain came down, the streams rose, and the winds blew and beat against that house; yet it did not fall, because it had its foundation on the rock. But everyone who hears these words of mine and does not put them into practice is like a foolish man who built his house on sand. The rain came down, the streams rose, and the winds blew and beat against that house, and it fell with a great crash."

(Matthew 7:24-27)

The importance of wisdom is emphasised by the following scriptures:

"My son, pay attention to what I say; listen closely to my words. Do not let them out of

your sight, keep them within your heart"
(Proverbs 4:20-21)

"For whoever finds me finds life and receives favour from the LORD."
(Proverbs 8:35)

"There is a way that seems right to a man, but in the end it leads to death."
(Proverbs 14:12)

A Test for all Sacred Scriptures

The sacred Scriptures of any Faith must always be able to withstand criticism over hundreds or thousands of years, because the *'truth'* they are said to be proclaiming can only be attested as *'true'* with time apart from being defended by its adherents, also, this gives the time to test the truth of prophecies. The Bible has been thoroughly tested in this way, is standing firmly today, its truth has not been undermined, and it remains the world's bestseller.

The Church –the universal community

The whole concept of 'church' is frequently misunderstood – it is thought of. as a 'building' and as a place people go to for weddings, births and funerals. In fact, the word 'church' is a collective term referring to the community of Christian believers, and is nothing to do with a building, and in fact it meets in a variety of places such as a house, hut, hall, cinema, theatre, church building and the like. This Christian community has existed since the time of Christ to the present day. It is important to bear in mind that the word 'church' comes from the Greek 'ekklesia' which means 'assembly' or 'gathering'; it can be used to describe any gathering and is not limited to the Christian church.

The Christian 'Church' should be characterised by love that is shown in helpful and caring words where biblical truth is expressed with a clear, bold and humble attitude and matched with practical help. The Church, however, meets in a variety of buildings for worship and fellowship. The true nature of the church in the general population of many countries has been overlooked and misunderstood. Many consider the Christian faith to be irrelevant to their needs, too challenging to their lifestyle; others have dismissed it due to receiving false or distorted information. But the church has been founded by the Lord Himself to meet the needs of all people, and to enlighten them on God's plan for humanity and for them as individuals. Christians are commissioned to go into all the world to present the good news about the Lord Jesus Christ and make disciples. In fact, most churches have some form of outreach activity to take the message of love, faith, and hope to non-

Christians. It is most necessary to understand that the Church is an organism of God, not an organisation of man. Through it, God acts supernaturally and empowers those in it. If it becomes just an organisation of man, it is no longer the real Church.

Concerning the status of Christians, it is interesting to note that all true believers in the New Testament are referred to as saints or 'sanctified ones' who have been set apart by God for a particular calling. All true Christians do in fact belong to one universal Church. However, there are many different types of Church groupings with a vast number of names, and having a variety of Church meeting places, all of which may well cause some confusion to outsiders. Many of these types of Church groupings are bible-based, and their differences have come about due to an emphasis on one particular aspect of Scripture, lifestyle or tradition.

Joining a Church

When a person becomes a Christian, it is important that they seek the fellowship and support of other Christians through affiliation with a church. However, as there are many types of churches with a wide variety of names, a few recommendations are set out as guidelines below.

- Firstly, they should pray to God for guidance

as to where He wants to plant them.

- They could then speak to a Christian friend to find out about their Church.

- If possible, they should join a local church, but only after they have seen what it provides.

    Certain things to look for would include: a friendly welcome and acceptance; a teaching programme for new Christians such as an Alpha Course, or similar.

- Bible-based teaching; a place that has prayer meetings; a place with the possibility of developing Christian friends; a place where you can grow as a Christian and go on to serve God in some way.

- A Church that has a missionary outlook both local and overseas.

On a cautionary note, they should be wary of joining any church where the leader or leaders demand absolute allegiance to them, and/or claim that they alone have the whole 'Truth' and the final say when interpreting the Bible.

The Giftings Given to the Members of the Church

To equip the church to fulfil its mandate, God has provided a number of spiritual gifts given to believers. Some of these gifts are visible like 'healing', whilst others are more quietly expressed like 'hospitality'. It should always be remembered that these gifts are given for *'the common good'*, as stated in 1 Corinthians 12, and used to encourage believers and to reveal the power of God. However, people should be careful not to compare or judge that some gifts are of more value than others.

Also, there are ministry gifts of apostles, prophets, evangelists, pastors and teachers as shown in Ephesians 4:11-13.

Apostles

Jesus chose twelve apostles to be with him in his earthly ministry. These were called to be followers of Jesus, up to and beyond his resurrection. After his resurrection they focused particularly on prayer and teaching. The post of apostle was also applied more generally to some who were recognised as having special status among mature believers. The post did not include the gift of prophecy.

It is clear that some of the apostles spoke and wrote God's very words which became included in the Scriptures and are in fact a large proportion of the New Testament.

Prophets

Prophets, in the Old Testament, were people given messages having divine authority from God, messages concerning: predictions of the future; guidance and judgments. The O.T. prophets often used the phrase, "Thus says the Lord", followed by the words given to them by the Lord.

In the N.T. prophetic words were given through the apostles and recorded in Scripture, but the gift of prophecy is given to many Christians as seen in Acts 2:14-18.

> *"Do not put out the Spirit's fire; do not treat prophecies with contempt. Test everything. Hold on to the good"*
>
> *(1 Thessalonians 5:19-21).*

Prophetic words, therefore, should be tested; furthermore, the apostle Paul lays down a system of accountability whereby two or three prophets can speak, and others should carefully weigh what is said (1 Corinthians 14:29-40). It is important to bear in mind that the prophetic words given in the New Testament are not added to Scripture as that is already established and finished.

Concerning the role of different posts like: Preacher, Teacher, Evangelist, Pastor. There will always be some overlap in role.

Evangelist

Those who receive the special gifting of an evangelist will be enabled to communicate the Gospel in an effective way to others. The disciples were told by Jesus to *"make disciples of all nations,"* (Matthew 28:19) and this means that He wants us to be sensitive and obedient to His voice so that He can draw people to Himself. Also, it says *"you will be my witnesses"* (Acts 1:8), so we are each called through our lifestyle, attitude and words to be His witnesses of who the Lord is and what He has done for us personally.

To provide an opportunity to 'proclaim' the Gospel often means that first of all genuine love and practical care should be shown to the people we are trying to reach. This may entail considerable cost of time and money before we can share with them the love of God.

Pastor

A pastor is a shepherd who tends his flock and leads them to pasture to feed. So, a pastor keeps watch over those in his charge and sees that they are cared for, discipled and fed on the Word of God.[7]

Jesus said to Peter:

> *"Feed my lambs; take care of my sheep; and*

feed my sheep."

(John 21:15-17)

The lambs and sheep in this passage are commonly considered to refer to children of God which includes children and adults . The job of all the people covering the five ministries given in Ephesians 4 is:

> *"to prepare God's people for works of service, so that the body of Christ may be built up until we all reach unity in the faith and in the knowledge of the Son of God and become mature, attaining to the whole measure of the fullness of Christ."*

(Ephesians 4:12-13)

Teacher

A teacher, in this context, is one who teaches Biblical Truth to the Church. The Lord Jesus Christ Himself was the supreme teacher, and this is supported by numerous Scriptures where His unique ability to convey and illustrate truth is further substantiated by miraculous demonstrations.

A Pharisee named Nicodemus said to Jesus *"Rabbi, we know you are a teacher who has come from God."* (John 3:2)

Again, another Scripture says:

"The people were amazed at His teaching, because He taught them as one who had authority, not as the teachers of the law."

(Mark 1:22)

There is a warning given that teachers who do not obey the teaching they are giving will not enter the kingdom of heaven. (Matthew 5:19-20)

It follows, therefore, from these and other Scripture references that the character of a person who teaches Biblical truth should be one who has integrity; follows Biblical teaching in their lifestyle; graciously teaches Scripture using the Word of God as the only Word of divine authority; and endeavours to follow the way Jesus taught and lived.

Church Services

The format of church services varies but would usually consist of a time of worship, prayers, a time of preaching; a time of communion; someone to lead the service and someone to give notices. There is also an inclusive aspect to services, that many churches provide, where believers in the congregation can be invited to participate in a time of sharing or the use of a Holy Spirit's gift. The believers' participation is supported through the doctrine of 'The Priesthood of all Believers' is given below, however, the extent to which this is operated in church services will vary.

The Doctrine of the Priesthood of all Believers

The apostle Peter pictures the Church as a building constructed of living stones with Christ as the Chief Cornerstone. He also represents the congregation as a company of priests, consisting of all believers, a holy priesthood of royal lineage with Christ as the great King High Priest when they meet together. (1 Peter 2:5-9)[8] In the future this priestly role is extended to include ruling, as stated in Revelation 5:10 "we shall reign on the earth".

In the Scriptures recorded[8], there is a common theme of participation by believers in the congregation as led by God's Holy Spirit, with a caution given that *"everything should be done in a fitting and orderly manner."* This 'order,' however, should be God's order that may not necessarily be ours, so this calls for people to be sensitive to the leading of the Holy Spirit.

Practical Outworking

Each believer has an opportunity to be an active member of the church through choosing hymns/songs, giving a Bible reading, praying, giving a short word of testimony, and using the gifts of the Holy Spirit as they sense His leading. This participation should be by general invitation and the church leadership and the size of the congregation will determine its practice. For some churches this participation will be carried out in the house groups or cell groups of the church.

Elders & Deacons

In the early church two types of leadership role were recognised and appointed, namely - elders and deacons. These people were chosen from the local congregation of believers.

The qualities required for those who would be elders are summarised as follows:

- being above reproach,

- the husband of but one wife,

- temperate,

- self- controlled,

- respectable,

- hospitable,

- able to teach,

- not given to drunkenness,

- not violent but gentle,

- not quarrelsome,

- not a lover of money. (1 Timothy 3:1-7)

Elders must be able to manage their own family well and see that their children obey them with proper respect. They must not be recent converts and must also have a good reputation with outsiders.

Deacons are required to have similar moral and spiritual qualities, (1 Timothy 3:8-13), but they are not required to teach. It is to be borne in mind that not all churches follow this leadership structure.

Paul and Barnabas appointed elders in each church and, with prayer and fasting, and committed them to the Lord in whom they had put their trust. (Acts 14:23) The term 'elder', whilst clearly indicating spiritual maturity, may not always mean maturity in age.

The function of elders is given in 1 Timothy 3:1-7, and also it says that:

> *"The elders who direct the affairs of the church well are worthy of double honour, especially those whose work is preaching and teaching."*
>
> *(1 Timothy 5:17)*

Also, when leading a church, they are referred to as

'elders', suggesting the security of having more than one person

To clarify the roles of those given in Ephesians 4:11 and those of Elders and Deacons. The first set refers to giftings and function, and the Elders and Deacons fill the practical roles of how and when these giftings are used in the church.

Concerning people who can be appointed as deacons, the Scriptures concentrate on the quality of the person and their lifestyle similar in fact to those required for elders , but they are not required to teach (1 Timothy 3:8-13), or to wait on tables (Acts 6:1-8). However, in the 1 Timothy 3 passage it states that: *"A deacon must be the husband of but one wife and must manage his children and his household well."* So again, it indicates that a deacon should be male. (1 Timothy 3:8-13, Acts 6:1-8, Acts 7)

The Growth of the Church

Much has been written on this subject but given here are just a few salient points to consider.

> ... In Acts 6 we are told that the number of the disciples was increasing and this was at a time when they had particularly given their attention to prayer, and to the ministry of the Word of God (the Bible).

... Then we are told that the Word spread, and this was closely followed by opposition.

... Similarly, *"the word of God continued to increase and spread"* (Acts 12) and in the story told here we see there was persecution followed by earnest prayer and a miracle.

... Again, Scripture states that *"In this way the word of the Lord spread widely and grew in power"* (Acts 19) and this took place in the midst of opposition, miracles and prayer.

In these, and other stories of the early church, we see something of a pattern emerging, having the common factors of preaching the Word of God to unbelievers, and this is in some way mixed with opposition, persecution, miracles and prayer.

You may well ask the question, therefore, *"who has the responsibility for the growth of the Church?"* The answer is in two parts.

... We do our part of faithfully and 'fully' preaching and sharing (one to one), the Word of God to unbelievers, (Romans 10:14-15, 15:18-19) coupled with listening and co-operating with God in earnest prayer,

... God in His own time and way will do His part by building the Church and performing miracles, which may occur with opposition and persecution. (Acts 11:19-21; 13:46-52)

... However, in the final analysis, it is God who gives the increase. (Acts 2:46-47; 11:21; 1 Corinthians 3:6-9)

The spiritual growth of believers is more important than the numerical growth of the church and the two are connected. The maturity process of the Christian is not automatic, but can be likened in some ways to the growth of plants in the sense that they need nourishment and the right environmental conditions, and this comes about particularly by feeding on and living out the Word of God in their lives.

The Responsibilities and Tasks of the Church

The responsibilities and tasks of every person in the Church is listed below:

... To: worship God; give God sacrificial praise;

... Show God's love to others and have a humble attitude; read and obey His Word the Bible;

... Seek His Will for our lives;

... Pray personal prayers

... Pray for others.

... Pray in the Holy Spirit;

... Pray for healing.

... Confess your sins to one another.

... Encourage one another.

... Be hospitable.

... Give sacrificially to God of ourselves, our substance and talents.

... Love God.

... Show God's grace in our lives.

... Serve the Lord with humility.

... Live in the power and boldness of the Holy Spirit.

... Preach the whole council of God.

... Be His witnesses.

... Act as salt and light in the world.

... Be self-controlled, alert and wary of the devil's schemes.

...Get beside people.

... Live at peace with others, as far as it depends on you.

... Answer with grace and patience those who question our Faith.

... Overcome evil with good.

... Seek to glorify God in all that we do.

The Benefits of a new life

A deep-down desire in the heart of all people is to find peace and happiness in a turbulent and uncertain world. They also want to be assured that they can find the path to forgiveness for things they have done wrong against others, and God. They are also looking for acceptance and satisfying purpose in this life, and at the end, assurance that they will not be punished for their misdeeds in the afterlife, if they believe there is an afterlife. Well, all these quests are met in the best possible way when a person comes into the position of knowing God's salvation.

Let us begin by defining the word 'salvation', and the meaning given in the Oxford dictionary is: *"deliverance from sin and its consequences and admission to heaven, brought about by Christ"* [9]

This describes a very satisfactory and secure state for the person who claims to have been 'saved', and has entered into the benefits that spring from it. The benefits that come from salvation are many, but the basic ones being addressed here are belief, forgiveness, hope, joy and peace. Briefly, it means that those who are 'saved' have resolved their questions of belief and forgiveness, and have discovered the source of true hope, joy and peace.

So, it can be said that such people have placed their belief or trust, in the Lord Jesus Christ - the One who has made salvation possible; they have found the relief of knowing that they are forgiven sinners. Finally, they can now enjoy these benefits that are not dependent on such factors as earthly wealth, good health or pleasant circumstances.

Many people search for such benefits in every place except the place where they are guaranteed to find them. The benefits also include having *"an inheritance that can never perish, spoil of fade – kept in heaven"* (1 Peter 1:4) It must always be remembered that the Bible states very clearly that people cannot be saved *by* good works, but are saved *for* good works. (Ephesians 2:8-10, James 2:14-17) The very offer of eternal salvation can cause people to seek it. They can then discover that this can only be received through the Lord Jesus Christ who is the only One with the power and authority to save us. (Acts 4:12) The Bible shows us that we are in great need to be *'saved from'* the consequences of remaining in our natural and inherited state of sin.

Forgiveness

It is one thing to obtain forgiveness from another person, but what about seeking to obtain forgiveness from God. As people are not perfect in their behaviour, and the Bible tells us that we 'have all sinned', so we all need to get forgiveness from God because generally we have ignored Him and just lived to please ourselves. However, Jesus has made a way for us to obtain complete forgiveness, as outlined below.

The provision of forgiveness of sin that people can receive through Jesus has come at the very high price of his suffering and death on the cross, and his sacrifice has given people release from the power of Satan and has opened the gateway to life with the power and guidance of the Holy Spirit. Also, the whole process of forgiveness has enabled these people to be seen as acceptable and holy children of God.

Hope

Each true believer has the sure hope of resurrection, as confirmed by the following scripture:

> *"Brothers, we do not want you to be ignorant about those who fall asleep, or to*

> *grieve like the rest of men, who have no*
> *hope. We believe that Jesus died and rose*
> *again and so we believe that God will bring*
> *with Jesus those who have fallen asleep in*
> *him."* [10]

(1 Thessalonians 4:13-14)

The biblical word 'Hope', in the context in which it is used, has no element of uncertainty in it.

Joy

Joy is one of the nine fruits of the spirit:

> *"But the fruit of the Spirit is love, joy, peace,*
> *patience, kindness, goodness, faithfulness,*
> *gentleness and self-control. Against such*
> *things there is no law."*

(Galatians 5:22-23)

As we continue to develop our relationship with God, our spiritual joy increases resulting from *"the joy of faith"* (Philippians 1:25), and *"the rejoicing of hope".* (Hebrews 3:6) It becomes a part of the Christian's character and experience, and helps to sustain them through the trials of life.

Also, we find joy in the attributes of God and receive benefit and advantage not only from his power, wisdom, truth, faithfulness, goodness, grace and mercy, but even in His justice and holiness. Isaiah looks forward to the time of Christ when believers will be seen as though they had not sinned.

> *"Of the increase of His government and peace there will be no end, upon the throne of David and over His kingdom, to order it and establish it with judgement and justice from that time forward, even forever. The zeal of the Lord of hosts will perform this."*
>
> *(Isaiah 9:7)*

In addition, the everlasting love of God is a matter of joy to believers (Psalm 30:4-5, Psalm 103:17, Jeremiah 31:3) Believers are also told to rejoice that *"their names are written in heaven".* (Luke 10:20)

Peace

The peace that Scripture refers to is not the peace that people experience when they are free from trouble, persecution and war, nor does it involve enjoying a good measure of prosperity and happiness. Pleasant as these would be, what we are referring to here is the spiritual peace of mind and soul. This peace is *"... from God our Father and from the Lord Jesus Christ".*[11] (1 Corinthians 1:3),

All people need peace with God, and this is made available to all true believers through Jesus Christ, and the Scripture states, *"... we have peace with God through our Lord Jesus Christ."* (Romans 5:1-2)

In Hebrew, 'peace' is *shalom*, and the equivalent in Greek is *eirene*. It has been said that this word does not mean 'absence of strife' or 'tranquillity of mind' but rather wholeness, health and completeness. This peace is shown by a calmness of spirit resting on God's character and promises, through rough and smooth times alike. It can be experiences only by God's grace as a gift.[12], It also results from right relationships with God and others.

Directions for the journey

As an introduction to this subject matter, it is worth considering that *Knowledge* is what we know, and *Wisdom* is the right application of what we know.[13] The Book of Proverbs provides practical wisdom for all aspects of life where decisions are important and life changing. In Matthew, Jesus Christ gives a clear warning to people not to just hear His words, but to put them into practice, or suffer certain consequences.

> *"Therefore whoever hears these sayings of Mine, and does them, I will liken him to a wise man who built his house on the rock: and the rain descended, the floods came, and the winds blew and beat on that house; and it did not fall, for it was founded on the rock.*

But everyone who hears these sayings of
Mine, and does not do them, will be like a
foolish man who built his house on the sand:
and the rain descended, the floods came,
and the winds blew and beat on that house;
and it fell. And great was its fall."

(Matthew 7:24-27)

If anyone is going to learn about any subject, they must be prepared to admit, if only to themselves, that they are lacking in knowledge in that subject and have a desire to know about it. Hence, having the right attitude is most important; the following sayings bear this out – 'If you are not teachable, you're not reachable' and 'learning requires submission'. To be wise, we should accept instruction; however, the way of the fool seems right to him. But we should not ignore God's discipline, and we should not lose heart, because He disciplines those He loves. If we are not prepared to accept the discipline of a loving father, we have become unreachable, and therefore, unteachable.[14]

Some people want to learn whilst others are happy to live in a less structured, more relaxed fashion, and perhaps are less academic and more practical in their outlook on life. But whatever outlooks, abilities and backgrounds we have in life, it is important for us to realise that there are a minimum number of things to know and consider about life. The essential things everyone should know about concern the guidelines that determine the direction their lives take, and the destination this could lead to.

These guidelines may be followed almost unknowingly from our families and those around us, or can be adopted willingly, from family members or others. The guidelines are usually in the form of a lifestyle that evolves through circumstances and ambitions, or a lifestyle that results from following a Faith. Whatever type of lifestyle is adopted, it will have a bearing on our character and destiny.

Hence, it is very important that a person receives the type of 'teaching' and 'guidance' that leads to a fulfilled life, having an assured hope and prospects of eternal life with God.

Teaching

In Acts 1:1 the writer refers to:

> *"all that Jesus began to do and to teach until the day he was taken up to heaven, after giving instructions through the Holy Spirit to the apostles he had chosen."*

From this Scripture it is interesting to note that the do comes before the teach, and this was true of so much of Jesus' lifestyle; his actions preceded so much of his teaching and were also an integral part of it. For example, soon after Jesus had called his disciples, he started his ministry with action by going to a wedding and changing their water into wine (John 2:1-11). The purpose for this action is shown in verse 11 - *"He thus revealed his glory, and his disciples put their faith in him."*

In many Scriptures we see the coupling of actions and teaching, as in we read that He was:

> *"... teaching in their synagogues, preaching the good news of the kingdom, and healing every disease and sickness among the people."*
>
> *(Matthew 4:23)*

He then proceeds to speak the words recorded in Matthew 5-7, commonly referred to as 'The Sermon on the Mount'. Another instance of this combined approach is given in Luke 5:17-26 where people brought a paralytic man to Jesus who, recognising their faith in Him, announced that the man's sins were forgiven, and he was healed. But the Pharisees questioned these actions because they did not recognise Him as God.

In Mark 11:15-17 we see Jesus driving out those who were buying and selling in the temple, after which he proceeded to teach his followers. The action of Jesus in prayer caused the disciples to say, "Lord teach us to pray," and He then gave them 'The Lord's Prayer' (Matthew 6:9-13, Luke 11:1-4), we note that the the extend and in some translations the words differ.

A unique feature of Jesus' teaching, which is mentioned in a number of Scriptures, is that *"He taught as one who had authority"*[15] He used this authority when he warned people against teaching as doctrine the rules of men. (Matthew 15:9, Mark 7:7)

It is apparent through his ministry that Jesus taught with compassion, and showed that he cared about people, and that his strongest words of rebuke were mostly reserved for religious leaders because of their pride, self-righteousness and hypocrisy.

Methods of Teaching used by Jesus

He taught through his actions and lifestyle, and also through direct speech and parables. The direct or straight teaching was given to His disciples and this was well illustrated with common objects and life situations. He also related His teaching to the common sayings and thinking of the day with words such as:

> *"... you have heard that it was said 'do not commit adultery'. But I tell you that anyone who looks at a woman lustfully has already*

committed adultery with her in his heart."

(Matthew 5:27-29)

Parables

The Universal Bible Dictionary edited by A.R. Buckland states: A parable is a narrative, imagined or true, told for the purpose of imparting a truth.[16]

Jesus taught the people by using parables, and when the disciples asked him why he did this, he replied, "The knowledge of the secrets of the kingdom of heaven has been given to you, but not to them." (Matthew 13:10-11) In a number of passages of Scripture, Jesus states that He speaks to the people in parables, but He will explain them to the disciples.[17]

In Hosea God states:

"I spoke to the prophets, gave them many visions and told parables through them."[18]

(Hosea 12:10)

There are many parables told in the Gospels, but most are found in the Books of Matthew and Luke, well known ones being:

- The Sower - Matthew 13:3-23, Mark 4:3-20, Luke 8:4-15.

- The Unforgiving Servant - Matthew 18:23-35.

- The Good Samaritan - Luke 10:25-37.

- The Prodigal Son - Luke 15:11-32.

- The Vine - John 15:1-8.

Guidance

The concept of God guiding and leading His people is a very important issue in the lives of believers, and the Bible provides us with many stories and statements of the ways that God guides. From these stories and statements many Scriptural truths and principles can be extracted. Guidance and leading from God are received in a number of ways including:

- Checking a response to a question, by using the expression: 'Prayerfully knocking' on doors'.

- Miracles, and words of knowledge.

- Prayer and waiting on God.

- Reading the Bible, and being convinced that God, by His Holy Spirit, has spoken to you.

- When you highlight a passage of Scripture for you to accept and act on.

Romans 8:14 states, *"those who are led by the Spirit of God are sons of God"*. Being led in this way implies commitment and obedience, meaning that the mind is to be spiritually focused and ready to do God's will. Romans also says:

"... those who live in accordance with the Spirit have their minds set on what the Spirit desires"

(Romans 8:5-6)

That is, following God's word and the Spirit's prompting. We don't decide God's plan for our lives – we discover it through listening to His voice and obeying it. (Isaiah 30:20-21)

The person of the Holy Spirit has a key role in guiding God's people. Being led by God's Holy Spirit implies commitment and obedience, and below are Scriptures which show things revealed and people led by Him. In Matthew 4:1 Jesus was led by the Spirit into the desert; and in Luke 2:25-26 Simeon had it revealed to him that he would not die before he had seen the Lord's Christ.[19]

We assert that God is sovereign and can do what He likes, when He likes, but He still asks Christians to exercise faith, follow the lead of the Holy Spirit and thus provide Him with further opportunities to show Himself as the only God of mercy, love, grace and power. If faith is not exercised and the Holy

Spirit is not listened to or obeyed, then all that people outside the Faith see are ceremonies, words and actions that are not empowered by God, and which therefore, achieve little or nothing that was intended.

If a person seemingly achieved something for God without depending wholly on Him through waiting on Him in prayer, then they weren't led by His Holy Spirit, and achieved nothing for Him. It is not uncommon for things to happen in our lives which we wish had not occurred and we didn't understand, yet later realise were for our good and our maturity as Christians. When these things occur, we must learn to be patient and trust God. When the going is tough, the Lord guides us through sign posts and corrections along the way, allowing us to see, hear and correct our path.

On a journey through the jungle the guide might say words to this effect - *"There is no path, I am the path, so follow me."* God says that He will lead the blind by ways they have not known, and that He will turn the darkness into light, and make rough places smooth. (Isaiah 42:16) Similarly, when people are 'lost' Jesus knows the way.

It is encouraging to remember that Jesus has promised that if His people listen for His voice, He will call them by name and lead them. Rest assured, He knows the best way that people should take because He said, *"I am the way and the truth and the life"*. This statement makes the claim that He is the Way to God, the Truth about God and the Life of God.

Another example of the way God guides us is in the story of how the Israelites were led from slavery in Egypt under Pharaoh to the 'Promised Land'. This came about because God enabled Moses to bring a number of miraculous signs and wonders to Pharaoh and the Egyptian people causing them grief. When the people were allowed to leave, God did not lead them along the short route, through the Philistine country as that would discourage them, but took a longer route through the desert, with much testing of their faith to trust Him. The full story is found in the Book of Exodus. This is the approach He often takes with those who are seeking to follow Him.

The Christian life can be very easily overloaded with 'activity' of all sorts, but time is needed to reflect and spend time with God. (Mark 6:30-32) At times God allows His people to go through difficulties and pain, and this is not because He enjoys doing so, but because He wants them to attain more of the characteristics of Jesus, and we can liken these difficulties to a piece of metal that is heated so that it can be shaped - more into his likeness.

It is due to His intense love that He allows us to go through trials, mistakes, disappointments and things that seem to go wrong, but it must always be remembered that God takes a long-term view of our lives, and His mind is set on transforming us more into His likeness.

Yes, God loves us as we are, but loves us too much to leave us as we are. Also, He is more concerned with our developing a godly character, than what we can *do* for Him. There are many Scriptures that relate to this theme, for example Romans 8:29 which indicates that He wants us, *"to be conformed to the likeness of His Son"*. For this to happen, every believer must listen to the leading of His Holy Spirit, and obey, even when we don't understand. Also, we must learn to be dependent on Him, and that calls for humility.[20]

Guidance through Miracles

Many miraculous interventions by God have occurred throughout history and still occur in the present day. A few examples from the Bible are listed below:

- The Flood - Genesis 6-8, Matthew 24:37-39.

- Moses spoken to through the burning bush - Exodus 3.

- The deliverance of the Hebrews from slavery in Egypt - through plagues, - Exodus 6-12.

- God tells Elijah there will be no rain until He says so, and feeds Elijah by ravens - 1 Kings 17-18.

- The healing of Hezekiah -see 2 Kings 20:1-11.

- The handwriting on the wall in Belshazzar's palace – Daniel 5.

- The swallowing of Jonah by a fish – Jonah 1:17-2:10.

The many miracles recorded in the O.T. by such notable figures as Joseph, Moses, Joshua, Samson, Elijah, Elisha, and Daniel.

- The birth of a son to Elizabeth who was barren – Luke 1:5-16, 57.

- The Virgin birth of Jesus Christ – Luke 1:26-38.

- The star that guided the wise men to the infant Jesus – Matthew 2:1-12.

- The transfiguration of Jesus – Luke 9:28-36.

- The numerous miracles performed by Jesus and recorded in the four Gospels.

- The lame man for thirty-eight years healed by Jesus - John 5:5-9.

- The paralysed man healed and the teachers of the law had their thoughts read by Jesus - Mark 2:3-12.

- The Resurrection of Jesus - Luke 24, John 20.

- The Ascension of Jesus - Luke 24:50-52, Acts 1:4-11.

- The Holy Spirit comes at Pentecost - Acts 2:1-4.

- The judgement of Ananias and Sapphira - Acts 5:1-11.

- The blinding of Saul - Acts 9:3-9.

- The freeing of Paul and Silas from prison - Acts 16:19-40.

- The healing miracles performed by Peter and Paul recorded in Acts.

- The cripple from birth healed through Peter - Acts 3:1-8.

- The vision given to Peter causes him to go to the Gentiles - Acts 10:9-35.

Guidance Through Visions

A vision from God provides a person with a 'sense of seeing' or receiving, a message from Him. In Acts 9:10-12, God revealed His message to Ananias in a vision and he acted on it, as shown further in the story. Another example is where the apostle Paul, receives a vision from God and acts on it (Acts 16:9-10). Also, in Acts 26:19 Paul asserts that *"he was not disobedient to the vision from heaven"*.

It follows that visions from God can be received in various ways: a strong impression of a message or picture which comes into a person's mind; or the highlighting in a person's mind of a word, phrase or picture when reading a biblical scripture. This word/action should be tested or confirmed before it is acted on, and it should always aim to glorify God and be in line with His purposes.

Habakkuk was given a vision and he waited on God for direction, and had to learn to wait for God's timing. This is often a painstaking process which may be likened to developing film from a camera, from misty to sharp (Habakkuk 2:1-3).

Jeremiah was given words of warning about false prophets, and God posed questions to these prophets:

> *"But which of them has stood in the council*
> *of the LORD to see or to hear His word? Who*
> *has listened and heard His word?"*
>
> (Jeremiah 23:16-22)

When God gives His people a vision or dream, they often want to see the resources in place before they make a start, but if the vision is of God, then He expects them to move by faith and then the resources will be provided.

Fellowship and Support in Trials

Fellowship

There are those who prefer their own company for most of the time, but the vast majority of people prefer to share their lives with others in companionship, friendship and love. They want to communicate and be part of a group - to belong.

The sad situation for many is that for various reasons they suffer loneliness. The good news is that for these, and those who desire a level of friendship, the Christian Faith can meet this need of friendship at a deeper level. The friendship that can come through Christians is special because it is a true sharing and bonding of hearts that comes through a common relationship that they have with the Lord Jesus Christ, and this is referred to as

Christian fellowship.

The friendship and support of other Christians requires them to:

- Love one another - John 13:34-35

- Depend on one another - Romans 12:4-5

- Honour one another above themselves - Romans 12:10

- Accept one another just as Christ accepted them - Romans 15:7

- Care for one another - 1 Corinthians 12:25-26

- Serve one another in love - Galatians 5:13

- Submit to one another - Ephesians 5:21

- Encourage one another - 1 Thessalonians 4:18

- Confess their faults to one another - James 5:16

- Pray for one another - James 5:16

- Offer hospitality to one another - 1 Peter 4:9

Support in Difficult Times

Difficulties come to all people, those of every Faith or no Faith, and subject them to a time of testing. These tests or trials can occur through their own actions, through the actions of others, or the reason may be unknown. However they come, they cause a range of responses from anger or revenge to bewilderment or resigned acceptance.

In such situations, it is good to get support and understanding from those who have had similar experiences. Through these difficulties which Christians encounter, God's purpose is to transform their character to be more like his. The difficulties are inevitable, and often arise as a result of their lifestyle being different from those around them. As they grow in their Christian lives, their priorities change and they begin to want to live to please God and do whatever is necessary to fulfil God's will for their lives'. These higher moral and caring standards act as a challenge to others, and can thus lead to testing of character, trials and suffering, and this is well illustrated by the apostle Paul:

We are hard-pressed on every side, yet not crushed; we are perplexed, but not in despair; persecuted, but not forsaken; struck down, but not destroyed - always carrying about in the body the dying of the Lord Jesus, that the life of Jesus also may be manifested in our body. For we who live are always delivered to death for Jesus' sake, that the life of Jesus also may be manifested in our mortal flesh."

(2 Corinthians 4:8-11)

In the story of Jesus in a boat with his disciples when a storm arose Mark 4:35-41, there is clearly support for the disciples and also a challenge for them to trust him in difficult times. So, it can be said that Jesus brings comfort out of chaos, rest out of rage, and faith out of fear.

Tests that people go through can be financial when they are faced with giving to others when their own needs are a high priority, and in these times decisions on giving should only be made after praying it through and remembering that the Lord is no man's debtor and will meet our needs according to his riches.[21]

The believer subjected to testing

All believers will experience testing of their character, discernment, judgement and actions. In this way God reveals to them how Christ-like they are, and how much they need to depend on Him for their sanctification. The apostle John reminded believers that *"... the one who is in you is greater than the one who is in the world."* (1 John 4:4). When Samson was tested he showed he was no longer dependant on God's strength. He trusted in himself, his strength, and did not seek God's help against his and the people's enemy, the Philistines, failed the test, and died in the process.[22] (Judges 16:17-20)

The Believer subjected to Trials

In fiery trials God has his hand on the thermostat, because he knows the heat required to burn away the impurities that hinder His purposes in our lives. An example of this would be a father who disciplines his child as he thinks best, but God disciplines us for our good, resulting in pain at times, but with the purpose of changing us into a godlier character. (Hebrews 12:10-11, 1 Peter 4:12; 5:10)

The severity of trials experienced by believers will vary from a testing of patience to being condemned to death by persecutors for their faith. An example of this testing is found in the story of Joseph because he suffered more than all his brothers, and it was his character that sustained him through years of betrayal, temptation, accusation and imprisonment. The level of a person's assignment determines the level of Satan's attack. He understood this when he looked back and saw how God had led him. Therefore, he was able to say to his brothers:

"Don't be afraid. Am I in the place of God?

You intended to harm me, but God intended it for good to accomplish what is now being done, the saving of many lives."

(Genesis 50:18-20)

So let us remove anything that hinders, or causes us to deviate from, God's priorities for our lives. As the Scripture says:

"Therefore, since we are surrounded by such a great cloud of witnesses, let us throw off everything that hinders and the sin that so easily entangles, and let us run with perseverance the race marked out for us. Let us fix our eyes on Jesus, the author and perfecter of our faith, who for the joy set before him endured the cross, scorning its shame, and sat down at the right hand of the throne of God."[23]

(Hebrews 12:1-2)

Testing

We are encouraged to *"give thanks in all circumstances"* and *"in everything give thanks: for this is the will of God in Christ Jesus concerning you."* (1 Thes 5:18, Acts 20:19) However, this may not always be easy.

Christians are meant to be Strong in the Lord. The Scripture John 15:5 clearly states that while we remain in a close relationship with Him, then our words and actions will bring glory to Him and achieve His ends. On the contrary, those things accomplished by us that do not depend on Him in any way, will not achieve anything spiritually.

Trials

Jesus told us to expect trials and troubles when we follow Him, it is part of the journey of faith, and he said to his disciples:

> *"I have told you these things, so that in me you may have peace. In this world you will have trouble. But take heart! I have overcome the world."*
>
> *(John 16:33)*

It is comforting to note that Isaiah notes that:

> *"... when you pass through the waters (of difficulty) that God is with us and that His people are precious and honoured in His sight."*
>
> *(Isaiah 43:2-5)*

We need to be reassured of this because we are forewarned that it is not *if* difficulties come, but when. The same thought is expressed in Jeremiah:

> *"But blessed is the man who trusts in the LORD, whose confidence is in him. He will be like a tree planted by the water that sends out its roots by the stream. It does not fear*

when heat comes; its leaves are always
green. It has no worries in a year of drought
and never fails to bear fruit."

(Jeremiah 17:7-8)

Suffering for Christ and the Gospel

In seeking to proclaim and maintain the truths concerning the Lord Jesus Christ, and the whole truth concerning the Gospel message there is often opposition from both the world and from some sections of the established Christian community. This should not be considered surprising as Christ told us to expect such treatment.[24]

Support for the weak and those who suffer

Throughout the Bible we see that God supports the weak and shows compassion to those who suffer, and so calls on His followers to do the same.[25] To those who are hurting, damaged or broken-hearted, God knows and shows compassion. As the psalmist writes *"He heals the broken-hearted and binds up their wounds."* (Psalms 147:3) And they can be further encouraged by the words in Psalms 34 where David exhorts people to boast in the Lord, and makes many statements of encouragement to let the afflicted rejoice such as:

"... he sought the Lord, and he answered,
and delivered me from all my fears; he saved
him out of all his troubles; taste and see that

*the Lord is good; those who seek the Lord
lack no good thing".*

Also, it should be remembered that those who have gone through difficult times are in a position to bring comfort and support to those in difficulties.

Butterfly/Chrysalis Struggle

It has been found that if a butterfly, struggling to get out of its chrysalis, was helped by someone to escape then it would result in the butterfly being unable to fly because in the effort and struggle to emerge it develops the strength to fly. So, the helper, with the best of intentions, sadly caused it to have an early death. What we can learn from this is that people should be left to struggle through the process and difficulties that repentance brings, but let them know that you care and are praying for them. This approach applies to many of the difficulties we experience as Christians and working through these unwelcome situations will enable our faith to grow. It follows, therefore, that others should not interfere but support them in prayer and so allow them to mature.

Believers are called to persevere

They are frequently encouraged in the Bible to continue in the Faith and persevere in spite of difficulties; they are called on to show courage in adversity or pain, and are further called on to show determination, endurance and firmness with a gracious attitude, being patient towards all people and revealing a generous spirit:

> *"Be on your guard; stand firm in the faith; be men of courage; be strong. Do everything in love."*
>
> *(1 Corinthians 16:13-14)*

Believers should always remember that:

> *"God did not give us a spirit of timidity, but a spirit of power, of love and of self-discipline."*[26]
>
> *(2 Timothy 1:7)*

Holy Communion

There is only one act of remembrance Christians are called upon to observe and there are scriptures to remind people of this reflective and devotional occasion. The act of remembrance being referred to is commonly known as Holy Communion. This act of remembrance is incorporated into a Church service or is a separate Holy Communion service.

The Holy Communion service is also referred to as: The Lord's Supper (1 Corinthians 11:20) The Breaking of Bread service. (Acts 2:42 & 46)

This service is derived from a simple meal that Jesus Christ had with His disciples shortly before he

131

was crucified. It was during this meal that this special act of remembrance was requested by the Lord Jesus Christ as described in the following Scripture:

> "... and as they were eating, Jesus took bread, blessed and broke it, and gave it to the disciples and said, "Take, eat; this is My body." Then He took the cup, and gave thanks, and gave it to them, saying, 'Drink from it, all of you, for this is My blood of the new covenant, which is shed for many for the remission of sins. But I say to you, I will not drink of this fruit of the vine from now on until that day when I drink it new with you in My Father's kingdom.'"
>
> (Matthew 26:26-29)

These words were later taken by the Apostle Paul when he wrote to the Corinthian Church asking them to remember the Lord Jesus Christ in this way and reminding them of their significance when he said, *"For whenever you eat this bread and drink this cup, you proclaim the Lord's death until he comes."* (1 Corinthians 11:26) , and for a full statement of the service read 1 Corinthians 11:23-29.

In some branches of the Christian Church, however, this essentially simple but deeply significant service has been overlaid with much ritual and ceremony that can obscure its true meaning and application to people's lives, so the essential teaching that should come from this type of service is set out below.

The meaning of the Lord's Supper is rich, and the symbols used have great significance for Christians. The broken bread symbolises Christ's body being given for us when He died on the cross (John 19:31-36), and the poured-out cup of wine symbolises the pouring out of Christ's blood for us, and through this act, He has obtained forgiveness for our sin.

When participating in the Lord's Supper, and following Christ's invitation to *"take and eat ..."* (Matthew 26:26), we are taking the benefits of Christ's death to ourselves.

Jesus had spoken previously in a symbolic way about His death and what it meant when He referred to Himself as the *"bread of life...which I will give for the life of the world"* (John 6:48-51), and He continues in this symbolic manner by saying, *"unless you eat the flesh of the Son of Man and drink his blood, you have no life in you."* (John 6:52-54). This illustrates again the benefits we, as Christians, receive from His redemptive work on the cross.

The Scriptures show that participation in the Lord's Supper is an open and continual invitation to Christians when they come together. Jesus instructed his disciples, *"do this in remembrance of me."* (Luke 22:17-20) An indication that this may have been a weekly event, *"On the first day of the week we came together to break bread."* (Acts 20:7)

When Christians meet together for this event they come at the Lord's invitation and on each occasion, are reminded of Christ's redeeming love, that they are included in His family, and that the act of meeting together in this way is a sign of unity with one another and with him. The Corinthian scripture supports this aspect of unity, and shows that believers participate in the blood of Christ:

In the passage in Corinthians, Paul sets out the conditions that should pertain when Christians meet to celebrate the Lord's Supper, and asks them to break bread to remind them of the Lord's body pierced for them, and to take wine in remembrance of the Lord's blood poured out for them. When they do this, they proclaim the Lord's death until he comes. Also, All who take part should examine themselves before they eat of the bread and drink of the cup. (1 Corinthians 11:17-34)

Paul goes on to warn people against eating or drinking *"in an unworthy manner"* and this is further emphasised that they are reminded to examine themselves in respect of discerning the true nature of His Church - one united body. In which case if any person is not in a forgiven and restored relationship with God and others, then this should be put right first before they come to this service. If these things are not put right then, this person, and perhaps others, will not receive the benefit that can be expected from this special time of meeting with God.

Renew

It is a general principle in life that people age and their health deteriorates, and this principle can apply to people spiritually. When a person becomes a Christian, they begin a relationship with God and in time this should strengthen, but from the outset it will be attacked in various ways. Attacks can be in the form of doubts, negative and discouraging comments and experiences, so there will always be a need for spiritual renewal. All these factors seem to indicate that a spiritual leakage can be at work, so Christians need to develop a way of life that is continually dependant on God for His resources to renew them spiritually. This same principle relates to us in the physical realm in that we cannot rely on the food that we ate yesterday or last week to keep us nourished and in good health; it is an ongoing daily process.

Whilst our bodies are declining in health and ability over time, our spiritual life is being renewed every day, (2 Corinthians 4:16). Furthermore, our new nature is being *"renewed in knowledge after the image of its creator".* (Colossians 3:10) Also, there is a cautionary note given in Romans that our bodies should be offered as a living sacrifice so that believers do not conform to worldly patterns of behaviour, but instead follow the Apostle Paul's injunction to *"be transformed by the renewing of your mind."* (Romans 12:1-2)

Restore

Due to human weakness, Christians can fail God for various reasons, such as giving in to temptation or selfishness, or being guilty of cowardice or some other shortcoming. When the person becomes aware of their failure, they can feel depressed or dispirited, and can wonder if they should carry on? They may wonder if their relationship with God can be restored? In these quite common circumstances, however, there is good news – God is waiting to forgive and restore the relationship when that sin is confessed. (1 John 1:8-9)

God's heart is always to restore, rebuild, and straighten out people's lives that have strayed away from Him, and wish to return. Some of these thoughts are reflected in Jeremiah 18:3-4 where we see something of God's attitude and resulting action towards people who sin. We are given an analogy of the potter working at the wheel, and the pot is marred, and he does not discard it, but reworks it into another pot. This is like us when we

136

turn back to God in faith and repentance, He works on us again to reshape us as He desires.

Wholeness

It is a fact that people may suffer from a wide variety of illnesses and medical conditions throughout their lives, and that when they occur healing is required. There are many occurrences, however, where people deny that they have a health problem, and this is frequently true for things spiritual, where people think they are alright with God and have no need of 'healing'. Whilst a person remains in denial, not very much can be done, so they must be persuaded to face the problem of spiritual pride, or whatever the problem is, so that their relationship with God can be restored.

It is always good to know that help is available for the asking from God, and we shall see from the following statements concerning the word 'wholeness' that God's ultimate desire for us is to be 'whole' or 'complete'. Let us remember the words of Jesus Christ when He said to the sick - "what do you want me to do for you?". With these thoughts in mind let us look further at the word 'wholeness'.

According to Biblical scholars, there are a number of words which are used in the N.T. for 'whole' many refer to all; a lot; entire; complete. But one word of particular interest is the word that is used especially in the Gospels for making sick folk 'whole':

> Then He (Jesus) said to the man, 'Stretch out your hand." So, he stretched it out and it was completely restored, just as sound as the other.'"
>
> (Matthew 12:13 NIV)

In the Revised Standard Version (RSV) it reads:

> "Then He (Jesus) said to the man, 'Stretch out your hand.' And the man stretched it out, and it was restored, whole like the other."

There are many references in Scripture to Jesus making people 'whole' or completely healed whatever the condition, and as He is **The Creator God**, nothing is too difficult for Him.

Wholeness - Spiritual Maturity

It has been said that 'spiritual maturity' can be measured by where we put our trust. Is it in God, or people, or things such as science, education, possessions, traditions, or in ourselves?

God wants us to be dependent on Him for direction in life and not ourselves, and this requires the revelation of and submission to His Will. This means that we will use the energy and abilities we have been given to ultimately fulfil His purposes. For most people this will not mean being in full-time Christian work, but will entail listening for and obeying His voice.

For the majority of people spiritual maturity is a slow process, because our submission to His Will is partial and slow. We need to be *weak* in our own strength and *strong* in His. The need for this balance is seen in Paul's letter to Corinth where God says:

> *"my power is made perfect in weakness,"*
> *and Paul confirms that by affirming, "For*
> *when I am weak, then I am strong."[27]*
>
> *(2 Corinthians 12:9-10)*

Revival

There is a general tendency among people to want to be comfortable and to resist change. So, therefore, there is always a need to be spiritually re-ignited, fired up, to strive to know more of the power and character of God in their lives. This is not comfortable talk, it entails moving into unknown territory, so there is often a response: *"I'm alright where I am, thank you"*, or perhaps, *"I'm more spiritually minded than Mr X or Mrs Y"*. So as in the physical realm, whereby we are usually subjected to the principle of physical deterioration with age, so this principle can apply to us spiritually, leaving us in a place, where we need to be spiritually refreshed, and indeed revived.

Let us consider the words of Jesus:

"Again, I tell you that if two of you on earth agree about anything you ask for, it will be done for you by My Father in heaven."

(Matthew 18:19)

Let us bear in mind, God only wants hat is best for us, while having the long-term view in mind. But as people often struggle with 'needs' and 'wants', sometimes His answer to us is 'No' or 'Not now'

There seems to be a balance between the sovereignty of God and the responsibility of man, where revival is transported to earth on the wings of fervent, believing, intercessory prayer.[28]

"O LORD, I have heard thy speech, and was afraid: O LORD, revive thy work in the midst of the years, in the midst of the years make known; in wrath remember mercy."

(Habakkuk 3:2 AV)

Revival it seems, is related to holiness, so, holiness encourages revival. This may explain why we see so little true revival today. As times past, if people generally become less set aside for God, coupled with a falling away as stated for the End Times, may be the reason we see so little true revival today!

Endnotes

1: Isaiah 40:8, 1Peter 1:23-25, Matthew 24:35

2: Galatians 1:8-10 and 2 Thessalonians 1:6-9

3: Isaiah 61:1-2, Matthew 8:26-27, John 16:28, John 17, Galatians 4:4

4: Matthew 5 & 23; Romans 1:18-32; 1 Corinthians 6:9-11; 2 Corinthians 5:10; Hebrews 13:4; 2 Peter 2; Revelation 1:18

6: Isaiah 1:1-4, 1:10-11, 40:8, 55:10-11, Amos 8:1-6, 8:11-12.]

7: Acts 20:28-31, Hebrews 12:5-6

8: Romans 12:5-8, Romans 15:14, 1 Corinthians 12:7-11, 1 Corinthians 14:26-40, Ephesians 5:19, Colossians 3:16, 1 Peter 4:10.

9: 'The Complete Oxford Dictionary volume one, published by Oxford University Press in 2011

10: Acts 23:6; 24:14-15; Romans 5:1-5

11: Ephesians 1:2, Philippians 1:2, Colossians 1:2

12: Psalms 29:11, John 14:27, Galatians 5:22, 2 Thessalonians 3:16

13: Psalm 111:10, Proverbs 19:11, James 3:17

14: Proverbs 19:20; 12:15; 13:18, Hebrews 12:5-6

15: Matthew 7:29, Mark 1:22, Luke 4:22, John 2:18-22, John 10:17ff

3:16 Universal Bible Dictionary public domain

17: Matthew 13:16-18, Mark 3:23, Mark 4:10-13, Mark 4:33-34, Luke 8:9-11

18: 2 Samuel 12:1-7, Isaiah 5:1-7

19: Acts 13:2-4, 2 Peter 1:21

20: Romans 8;14-17, 2 Corinthians 4:8-11; 5:17.

21: 2 Chronicles 31:6-12, Nehemiah 9:16-25, Malachi 3:8-10, Philippians 4:19

22: Jud 3:1-4, 2 Chronicles 32:8-23, Jeremiah 6:27, 9:7, Daniel 1:12, Luke 8:13, Romans 12:1-2, 1 Corinthians 3:12-13, 2 Corinthians 2:9, Galatians 6:4-5, 1 Thessalonians 5:21, Hebrews 3:7-8, James 1:3, 1:12.

23: Psalms 37:32-33, Matthew 5:23-24, Mark 13:11, Luke 22:38, Acts 12:4-6, 16:37, 23:6, 2 Corinthians 8:2, 1 Thessalonians 3:2-3, 2 Thessalonians 1:4, 1 Peter 1:6, 2 Peter 2:9, Revelation 3:10.

24: John 15:18-21, Acts 5:41, 9:16, Romans 8:17, 36, 2 Corinthians 1:7, 2 Timothy 2:12, Hebrews 11:25, James 1:2-3, 1 Peter 2:20-21, 3:14, 5:10

25: Psalms 18:35, 37:16-17, 91:12, Isaiah 41:10, Matthew 11:28, Acts 5:41, 1 Corinthians 9:22, 2 Corinthians 4:7-18, Galatians 6:2, Philippians 1:29, 2 Timothy 1:7-8

26: Romans 11:22, Colossians 1:21-23, 2 Thessalonians 1:4, 1 Timothy 4:16, 2 Timothy 3:14, Hebrews 12:1-3, James 1:2-4

27: Jud 6:15-16

28: Luke 1:10-13, Acts 1:14-15, 4:24-31, 12:12-17.]

Chapter 4

Discipleship

This chapter requires the reader to make a choice to make a commitment for the 'best life'.

Fulfilling God's Will

As we see God's attributes, His character, and the miraculous provision He has made for all who believe and trust in Him, it only remains for people to respond to him and so find the hope, security and help for life here, and the assured everlasting destiny in heaven with a loving God. In view of this, let us carefully consider our response, because whilst there will be challenges and joys in becoming a Christian, it will also bring opposition to a change in lifestyle when a person begins to submit their will to God. At this point, it should be remembered that even the Lord Jesus Christ, God's Son, did not come on earth to do His Will, but that of His Father. Jesus said, *"I seek not to please myself but him who sent me"* (John 5:30), and this is the same commitment that God asks of those who become Christians.

So, to understand how this commitment can be made, people must know that the process of becoming a Christian entails submitting our will to the will of God. It follows, therefore, that nobody can begin to fulfil God's will until they become a Christian, and an explanation of this process is given later.

In plain words, God's Will is for us to *know* Him and be *led* by Him, and there is clear guidance given in the following Scripture:

> *"Trust in the LORD with all your heart and lean not on your own understanding; in all your ways acknowledge him, and he will make your paths straight."*
>
> *(Proverbs 3:5-6)*

He also wants us to mature – *"the Lord disciplines those He loves..."* (Proverbs 3:11-12)[1]

It is to be borne in mind that God has a personal plan for each of our lives, and this will be found when we submit to Him and discover *His Will* for our lives.

To discover God's will, we firstly need to hear God's words not just with our ears but in our hearts and thoughts, and people are called to be careful how they think because our lives are shaped by our thought.[2]

Opportunity and adversity

Life has its opportunities, adversities and obstacles; however, it seems that the opportunities that God gives mostly come with adversity or obstacles. An example of this is seen in the story of Joseph (Genesis 37-50) who reached a high and privileged position in the land of Egypt that was a blessing to his family, to the Egyptian people and others. But this only came about after he had gone through years of adversity and suffering. He obeyed God through the tough times, and the result was that God blessed him and made him a blessing to others. This surely is an example for all Christians.

Joseph could have sought revenge on his brothers for the bad treatment they had given him, but instead he reassured them:

> *"Don't be afraid. Am I in the place of God?*
> *You intended to harm me, but God intended*
> *it for good to accomplish what is now being*
> *done, the saving of many lives. So then,*
> *don't be afraid. I will provide for you and*
> *your children." And he reassured them and*
> *spoke kindly to them.*
>
> *(Genesis 50:19-21)*

The Will of God

You were born for a purpose. Your greatest challenge is to discover it and live in the centre of it. In spite of his failures, the Bible says, David had served God's purpose in his own generation (Acts 13:36). There is no greater testimony than that!

Before you find life's purpose, you often go through a series of adversities that cause you to let go of the temporal and grasp the eternal! For Paul that meant the loss of everything! (Philippians 3:8) Whatever our past, we are not perfect, we have all made a mess of things but, there is hope of a new start, a fresh horizon, a fulfilling purpose. So, it can be seen that it's not what we can do for God, but what God wants to do through us by the power of His Holy Spirit.

A Blockage to Fulfilling His Will

A number of things can bring about this blockage such as failing to forgive someone; following your way, and not following God's revealed way to you; being attracted to an alternative way of life; a negative change of circumstances that causes the person extreme disappointment and confusion; the illness or death of a loved one; or personal illness.

The Human Condition

When people begin to think about God, their first concern is often a consideration of their own character, the type of life they have lived, their present lifestyle, and perhaps a feeling of unworthiness to even approach God. However, God's first concern is whether or not a person knows Him and has a living relationship with Him. So, whilst the nature and characteristics of people can vary from being kind, gentle, thoughtful, or loving, to being selfish, cruel, thoughtless, hateful, or evil to one another, as far as God is concerned, no person is good, (Psalms 53:1-3, & Romans 6:23). He sees goodness in the person who knows Him and puts Him first in life and this is what we all fail to do.

The initial step in getting to know God is to be aware of how He sees us. The descriptions given in the Bible for the basic human condition, sadly, are not flattering, for it reveals that we all start out in life basically concerned about ourselves and what we want, and this means that we have ignored and/or disobeyed God's claim on our lives, and consequently we have failed to recognise Him as our Creator and have not submitted our lives to Him nor worshipped Him only as God Almighty.

This selfish attitude towards God in the Bible is referred to as 'sin'. The word 'sin' is often confused with 'sins', but the word 'sins' refers to acts, attitudes and thoughts which are abhorrent to God and are the result of 'sin'.

The word 'sin' basically means that the person through ignorance, or a rebellious spirit, has just lived to please themselves. They, and all people, have a need to be forgiven for ignoring the fact of God's love, when He died to pay the sacrificial penalty for all sin.

The Biblical scholars state that the word 'sin' in the N.T. Greek as meaning refers to 'a missing of the mark'. We have missed God's high standards, and cannot hope to even approach his standards, and these can also be thought of as people living selfish lives without reference to God, but either approach is an offence to God, when one considers what He has done for us. So a recognition of the above facts leaves all mankind in a position of dire need before God, and the process whereby a person can find forgiveness and new life is explained later.

In the early stages of thinking about matters of Faith, it is well to establish the basis on which the Christian Faith stands, and there are two approaches to consider, one is formal and the other is relational.

Formal Religion vs A Relational Faith

Followers, of any Religion, who only follow it in a formal way, with rules and practices, without having a relationship with a living God, will find that their faith is empty and they are separated from God. Whereas, a true Christian has a relationship with Christ, whether, a good or poor relationship, because that relationship is with the only Living God.

To those who follow a Religion in a formal manner can be defined as those who follow rules, codes of behaviour, conventions and ceremonies that relate to any religious or Faith group, including Christianity. In any formal religion *man seeks God* – seeks to find him, appease him, gain his favour, gain understanding, following a set of rules and ceremonies, but does not provide a personal interaction between the follower of a Faith and God.

Despite being utterly sincere, zealous, and their motives honourable, they rely on obedience to Scriptures, laws or customs to earn salvation or the means to obtain a better life in the future. But sadly, they will not find a spiritual life that connects them to a source of power which can change their character for the better and for the benefit of others or have assurance of eternal salvation.

However, they may well be able to achieve great areas of control in their lives and achieve great things through their endeavours, but their lack of a personal relationship with the central God of their Religion/Faith means that their Religion is powerless. This is because the personal connection to a living God is missing, and the only changes they can make are by their own efforts, that is, from the *outside, not from the inside, which is only possible by God.*

The danger of adopting a formal religion can be seen in a false sense of security and hope; a false view of thinking that sincere devotion and deep conviction are sufficient and right to justify any actions they take, even if they are harmful to others. A biblical example of this was the Pharisees who followed the Jewish Faith with great zeal and sincerity, and yet were responsible for the death of the Lord Jesus Christ.

However, in the Christian Faith there is the opportunity for a direct connection and interactive relationship to form between the believer and the living God, which provides the opportunity for prayers to be answered, and for God to speak to them through the Word of God, the Bible, thus developing further that relationship, and that will begin to change the person's character from the *inside to make them more like Jesus.* This living God *is seeking them first and waiting to speak to them* in varied ways to give love, guide, reveal truth, impart understanding, and challenge believers in many ways, encouraging them to grow in faith and trust. As shown later, the Christian Faith provides the security of a living Faith, that connects into God's vast resources of grace and power. It is worth noting the fact that when we are tested in a crisis, our character is revealed, so we should seek to develop a 'close walk with Jesus', if we wish to be a good Christian witness when in a crisis.

The 'Good News'

A clear distinction is made here between all other Faiths and Christianity. In other Faiths they seek after God, but in Christianity God seeks after us. This message is 'The Gospel Message' meaning 'The Good News' as taken from the Bible's New Testament. To meet the above basic human needs, people need to recognise that they have a need to be forgiven and get a right relationship with the living God, as revealed   through the Lord Jesus Christ, who, as God's Son is the source of the 'Good News', for in His life and character He showed us the very nature and heart of God. He:

- was miraculously born through a virgin Mary two thousand years ago;

- came and lived among ordinary people and became a carpenter, then called twelve disciples around him and started a preaching and teaching ministry;

- showed compassion through healing the sick and raising the dead;

- showed by His actions that he cared about and helped people whoever they were;

- showed that whilst He was concerned about the welfare of people's lives, and about their eternal destiny, and hence, provided a way whereby they could be eternally saved by believing that He was God's Son;

- taught His disciples, and later the apostles, to call people to confess that they had led selfish lives, pleasing themselves and ignoring His rightful claim on their lives – (this lifestyle is referred to as 'sin' in the Bible);

- was crucified to pay the penalty for the sin of everyone who trusts in Him for salvation;

- rose from the grave and ascended back to heaven;

- did all this so that those who believed and repented could be forgiven, empowered to live a new life and be assured of a place in heaven with Him when they die.

All the above was prophesied many years before through the Old Testament prophets.

So, from the above outline of the 'Good News' we can see that the Gospel message is based on the sobering reality of our need of God's forgiveness and of a new life.

It is very important to realise that this intimate gospel message comes from God who has shown His heart of love towards us and has made every provision for us, and this statement is supported by the fact that the Lord Jesus Christ whilst on earth showed a personal interest in people, and He has not changed because He still wishes to be in direct contact with us. Uniquely, this does not require the intermediary of a human priest, because our God is a loving, relational God and earnestly desires us to know Him personally, and hence, has done all that is necessary to provide for our personal salvation through the Lord Jesus being crucified for our sin. This means, however, that to attain salvation, we must first understand that in our 'natural' state, we are estranged from Him and a miraculous interaction needs to take place between God and us, enabling us to come to know Him personally, and this divine process is known as *'Conversion'*.

Conversion

The key distinguishing feature of the Christian Faith is that it operates through God's miraculous power and grace (undeserved love), and this requires our humble, thankful and repentant response. The first thing to understand is that a person cannot be born a Christian, and someone is not found to be acceptable or unacceptable based on whether their parents or family were Christians or not. Another common misunderstanding is that a person can become a Christian through doing good deeds, but unfortunately, this is not an option. People try to get right with God through doing good deeds, which is like trying to change themselves by following rules and regulations, and this relates to changing from the *'outside in'*, whereas God changes people's hearts and motives from the *'inside out'* as shown in Ephesians:

"For it is by grace you have been saved,
through faith—and this not from yourselves,
it is the gift of God—not by works, so that
no-one can boast."

(Ephesians 2:8-9)

The fact is that each person must always have a direct meeting with God — initially through recognition of the deity of the Lord Jesus Christ as God, coupled with confession and repentance. The process of Christian conversion starts in a personal way when a person first becomes aware that in God's sight all are guilty of committing sin, as explained earlier under the heading 'The Human Condition'. If people just want to please themselves in how they live, they are showing a rebellious attitude towards God, their Creator. This attitude is referred to as lawlessness (1 John 3:4), and refers to the failure of people to keep God's moral laws. The Scriptures further reveal that this failure to keep God's laws and preference for living to please ourselves, is due to an inborn weakness in all people, so all are guilty. They also have a need for a new start in life, and a need to know God personally and this requires trusting God, having the confidence to share their thoughts and life with Him. This is the challenge people are asked to make. Trusting God is put to the test when our circumstances change so that we can learn to depend on Him more for our guidance and security and not ourselves. As God spoke through the prophet:

"Forget the former things; do not dwell on the past. See, I am doing a new thing! Now it springs up; do you not perceive it? I am making a way in the desert and streams in the wasteland."

(Isaiah 43:18-19)

A real test of trusting in God is well illustrated by the example of tightrope walker Blondin who walked across the Niagara Falls on a tightrope, who then asked the people watching, *"do you believe I can walk across with a man on my shoulders?"* – silence - then his manager shows his trust/belief, and goes across on his shoulders, and he demonstrated absolute trust, and that is the type of trust we are expected to place in God. So, let us see how this important element of 'trust' relates to the Christian Faith and the Bible.[3]

We all meet unexpected trouble at some point in our lives, but how do we respond to it?

Do we just make the best of it; try to find somebody to blame; say it must somehow be my fault; sink into self-pity; or go and lay the whole situation before God in prayer, examine our hearts and seek his guidance? These situations are also an opportunity to grow in faith.

Becoming aware of a needy condition indicates that God's Spirit is interacting with our spirit. He is speaking to us and endeavouring to draw us to Himself in a relationship of love. To receive forgiveness of our sin, we must first understand that God has always demanded a blood sacrifice to pay the penalty for our guilt. In the times before Christ came, the Hebrew people were required to sacrifice an unblemished lamb to cover their personal sin, but the good news is, that when the Lord Jesus Christ came, He paid the ultimate blood sacrifice by dying on the cross. He was the only One who was able to pay the penalty for sin for all mankind because He alone was sinless. Having accepted the need for our sin to be forgiven and their our guilt to be removed, the next step is to respond by confessing and turning away from their sin, asking for forgiveness and thanking God that the Lord Jesus Christ, God's Son, has paid for their sin. Then, if these steps are taken, a transaction takes place between God and the person. This response is known as Christian Conversion and is also known as 'being born again', or 'being saved' and so the person begins a new, empowered life.

If this commitment is made with a sincere and humble attitude, and a repentant spirit, then God responds by cleansing us from sin and the guilt of sin from our past life. Also, He gives us the gift of the Person of His Holy Spirit who comes to live within us and empowers us to start living a new life - the Christian life in God's family. Taking this step of faith, does not mean that He wishes to control us like puppets but rather invites us to submit to Him as a loving Father, and their relationship to Him becomes that of His sons and daughters. It should be borne in mind that submission to God is not weakness, but wisdom.

The outcome of all this means that, from God's point of view, there are only two types of people in the world – the unforgiven sinner, and the forgiven sinner. So, it can be said that unless a person accepts the 'Bad News' of the need before a Holy God to be forgiven and cleansed, then they are not in a position to appreciate or receive the 'Good News' of God's forgiveness and an empowered, new life.

There are many passages of Scripture that contain the three basic conditions that have to be met and accepted for someone to obtain personal salvation, namely - repentance, belief and confession.

Repentance and Forgiveness

Repentance refers to a change of mind and attitude with regard to Jesus Christ God's Son, leading to a new direction in life. It involves regretting our past lifestyle and seeking God's forgiveness for the fact that we, like all people, are guilty. As the Scripture reveals, *"all have sinned and fallen short of God's glory"* (Romans 3:23), and this can be expressed by people just living to please themselves, and ignoring the very high price the Lord Jesus Christ has paid for their sin through his suffering and death on the cross. Part of this repentance process is recognising and accepting that God's Word, the Bible, is true and that we can rely on what it says and be confident that we have received His forgiveness and salvation when we repent.

Belief

Personal salvation centres around what we believe concerning The Lord Jesus Christ, and the basic essential beliefs for those of us seeking to come to God in repentance and faith is that we acknowledge that He alone is God Almighty who is our only Saviour and Redeemer. We must also accept that He is the only one who can save us eternally, and go on to thank Him for our salvation.[4]

Confession

There are two ways of confession: one informal and the other formal. The informal way relates to our everyday conversations where we share openly about our Faith in a natural way, as opportunities occur, where we are best advised to limit ourselves to answering only the point in question. Any further talk about the Faith should generally be by 'invitation only' from the other person(s). The words of 'confession' should be spoken with patience, in an attitude of humility and backed up by appropriate actions and lifestyle. Also, we should admit when we don't know the answer to a question. The formal method of confession relates to a public declaration of our Faith by giving a word of testimony to others, often in a prearranged setting, or when being baptised by immersion in a public place before a number of people.

Becoming a Christian

We have clear guidance from the Bible regarding this life-changing step. Jesus said *"I am the way and the truth and the life. No-one comes to the Father except through me"*. (John 14:6)

We will first need to recognise that our chief sin is that our present lifestyle is lived for ourselves and others, and that God is not at the centre of our lives which is in fact a rejection of Him. Having reached this point then, based on the information under the previous three headings, we will then need to do the following:

- Repent of our sin, and that means changing our minds towards God and regretting our previous lifestyle that was just lived to please themselves ourselves;

- Ask God for forgiveness,

- Believe on the Lord Jesus Christ as God's Son;

- Thank Him for dying to pay for our sin,

- Thank Him for the gift of the Holy Spirit who begins to live in them,

- Confess their faith to others.

When we are prepared to take these steps with sincerity, humility and a repentant spirit, then we can use a prayer like the one given below:

Lord Jesus Christ,
I know you died on the cross for my sin and
I want you to be the Lord of my life, now and
forever.

Please forgive me for the way I have sinned
against you by leaving you out of
my life and living only as I wanted.
I submit my life to you and thank you for paying
the penalty for my sin.
Thank you, Lord, for your forgiveness that I don't
deserve, and for giving me the Person of
your Holy Spirit to live in me.
With your help I will seek to love and obey you
as Lord of my life.

There is no exact set of words to make this commitment, but remember, whatever words we use God does not only hear the expression of our lips, but He reads the attitude of our hearts.

Now, tell someone what you have done. And if you have prayed this, or a similar prayer containing the above essential truths with sincerity, then, based not on your feelings, but on the authority of the Bible, you can state with confidence that God has saved you. Scripture tells us that:

"That if you confess with your mouth, 'Jesus
is Lord,' and believe in your heart that God
raised him from the dead, you will be saved.
For it is with your heart that you believe and
are justified, and it is with your mouth that
you confess and are saved."

(Romans 10:9-10)

This Scripture goes on to say:

> "Anyone who trusts in him will never be put
> to shame. For there is no difference between
> Jew and Gentile - the same Lord is Lord of all
> and richly blesses all who call on him, for,
> everyone who calls on the name of the Lord
> will be saved".

He has made you into a new person with a fresh start as attested to by the Scripture (2 Corinthians 5:16-17). So, He has started a personal relationship with us, He knows us and we are just beginning to know Him as is clear from the Scripture John 10:14-15. The sheep know His voice. It should always be borne in mind that there is no other name through whom a person can to be eternally saved (Acts 4:12).

It is to be remembered that Jesus taught his disciples, and others, and that all Christians should receive teaching about the biblical Scriptures and the Christian life from Holy Spirit led teachers.

Other benefits the new Christian will receive include hope, joy and peace.

Hope: The biblical word 'Hope' in the context it is used, has no element of uncertainty in it, and this truth is further confirmed in 1 Peter 1:3-4, where it states that our new birth comes with a living hope through the resurrection of Jesus Christ, and we also receive a glorious future of an inheritance that can never perish, spoil or fade that is kept in heaven for us .

Joy: We read in the Scriptures of *"the joy of faith"*, and *"the rejoicing of hope"* (Philippians 1:25, Hebrews 3:6) and it enters very much into the Christian's character and experience, and is special to believers in Christ. In addition, the everlasting love of God is a matter of joy to believers (Psalm 30:4-5, Psalm 103:17, & Jeremiah 31:3). True believers are also told it is a matter of joy that, *"... their names are written in heaven"* (Luke 10:20).

Peace: The peace that scripture refers to is not the peace that people experience when they are free from troubles, persecution and wars, and could be enjoying a good measure of prosperity and happiness. Pleasant as that is, but what is being referred to here, is the peace we get from God, spiritual peace of mind and soul. This peace is *"from God our Father and from the Lord Jesus Christ"* (1 Corinthians 1:3, Ephesians 1:2, Philippians 1:2, & Colossians 1:2).

It must always be remembered that becoming a Christian will bring opposition and difficulties from some people, as Jesus said. So, we have to learn to trust Him for the grace, wisdom and strength to get through tough times, with support from other Christians.

Steps into the Christian Faith

The spiritual journey into the Christian Faith can be summarised in six steps:

- Calling – you feel there must be more to life than what you've experienced so far, so you begin to turn to God for answers.

- Concern – you're troubled and must find out the truth about the Christian Faith.

- Conviction – a battle of wills, and you know what you ought to do.

- Conversion – you repent and believe in Jesus Christ as God's Son and Saviour.

- Consolidation – you seek to advance in understanding and spiritual growth.

- Continuation – you continually seek to be a good witness and serve God.

Evidence of Christian Conversion

After this 'conversion' experience has taken place, our character begins to change little by little, to make us more and more like the character of The Lord Jesus Christ. Some of these miraculous changes are outlined below - given in no particular order:

- We want others to know and experience what we have received from God: acceptance into God's Kingdom, forgiveness of sin, cleansing from guilt, joy, fellowship with God and other believers; a purpose in living and the power to live a new life.

- We want to worship and praise God. They We want to share God's love with others.

- We want to pray – to commune with our Father in heaven, and hear what He has to say to us through the Bible. They We want to read His Word the Bible. We want to meet together with other Christians to enjoy one another's friendship and fellowship.

- We want to live pleasing to God - finding and fulfilling His will for our lives resulting in the fruit of God's Spirit being seen by positive changes in attitude and lifestyle.

- We want to receive from God whatever spiritual gifts He has for us, and use them to bring honour to Him and benefit to others.

From the above list, it can be seen that the motivation for living the Christian life is not out of a sense of duty or fear, but out of a response of love for God and the change he has empowered us to bring about in our lives.

It should be noted that the extent to which the above changes take place, will depend on a number of factors including the person's walk of faith and obedience to the will of God. As the Christian matures, more of the above changes will be realised. It will be observed that none of the above characteristics are 'natural' but supernatural, and hence, it is not within our power or ability to effect these changes in attitude or lifestyle, nor can we take credit for them. We can only thank God for His love, grace and help for others and ourselves.

Glorious Freedom

When we become Christians, He provides freedom from the power of sin, and freedom from religious customs, practices and rituals devised by man - not ordained by God. Indeed, God has *not* required us to:

- worship Him in a particular type of building;

- contact Him through an intermediary such as a priest;

- work for our personal salvation;

- fulfil any particular duty (other than to obey Him and seek to fulfil His will for our lives) or ascetic lifestyle;

- worship any other person or thing besides Him;

- use icons, idols or statues of any kind;

- partake in elaborate ceremonies or processions;

- wear any special type of clothes;

- change or mutilate our bodies in any way;

- take up arms to defend the Bible or the Christian Faith;

- pray at any particular time, or frequency, day or night;

- pray using any particular form of words, except that we should include the model prayer that the Lord Jesus Christ gave us (Matthew 6: 5-13) - its frequency is not indicated.

Nobody is required to fulfil the above conditions as a way of earning salvation or merit, because it must always be remembered that good works of any kind cannot earn salvation – it must be received through faith in the sacrifice of Christ for our sin, as a free gift, or not received at all. Rather, good works are meant to follow salvation.

Let us remember that whilst all the resources of God are made available to us through our relationship with Him, we must learn to trust and rely on Him to meet our needs. So, when we sin by going our own way instead of God's through disobedience, or failing to trust or rely on Him, then they we should not blame God because His resources are always available. The good news is that through confession and repentance, we can be forgiven and restored to fellowship with God as stated in 1 John 1:9.

God's Conditional Outcomes

God's offer of being accepted by Him, knowing Him and receiving the gift of eternal life comes with the conditions of us recognising that there are first the matters of belief and repentance to be accepted and acted on by us. Also, it should be borne in mind that God "... *wants all men to be saved and come to a knowledge of the truth*" (1 Timothy 2:4). So in His kindness He warns us "... not to show contempt for the riches of his kindness, tolerance and patience" (Romans 2:4-5) or we face His just judgement.

It is important to remember that we all start life as

sinners in God's sight, and the problem of sin can be simply explained as people just living to please themselves without reference to God. However, some erroneously think that following a religious code of rules, doing good works and kindly deeds, will be acceptable to God and give them a place in heaven, but it will not.

To avoid this judgement the Lord Jesus Christ has died to pay the punishment for the *"... sins of the world"* (1 John 2:2) for all those who have submitted their lives to Him. We are re-assured that *"God so loved the world ..."* (John 3:16-18)

It is noteworthy that in the above Scripture the word *'perish'* is associated with God's Judgment and has great significance. It is used to describe a very serious final state of existence that a person comes into when they die not having accepted the Lord Jesus Christ as their personal Saviour.

It is out of a heart of love that God warns people who are sexually immoral, thieves, drunkards, slanderers or swindlers, that they will not inherit the Kingdom of God (1 Corinthians 6:9-11).

However, there is hope here because this text goes on to state, "and that is what some of you were". But through repentance these people were forgiven and enabled to live the Christian life, and so can we today. Regarding our good works and kindly deeds, it's not that He does not want to see them, He welcomes them, but does not accept them as a means of earning eternal salvation, because it cannot be earned (Ephesians 2:8-9).

Love - Towards God and Man

There needs to be something said about 'love' in the Christian Faith, because over the years the word 'love' has been misused, abused, corrupted and misunderstood. It has been used when lust was intended; as a means to achieve selfish aims, as well as to flatter or deceive. Children who grow up in a dysfunctional family, where they are abused mentally and/or physically, where they are not wanted, where the parents split up, or where there are a number of partners, will be deeply scarred and have a high probability of not understanding the true meaning of love.

Some parents interpret love to their children as giving them most or all of what they ask for; this means that neither parent nor child understands the true nature of love. A wise parent knows when to give and when to say 'no' – for the child's own good and for their character development.

So, if people want to understand the true meaning of love, then they need to consider the life and death of the Lord Jesus Christ. For example, the quality of His love entailed showing compassion and giving practical help to those in need, showing 'tough love' when required, and in the end demonstrating that it was sacrificial, unconditional and selfless when He died on the cross for the sin of others.

It is very important, therefore, that we follow in His footsteps through observing Scriptures (Isaiah 58:6-12, Matthew 25:31-46 & Colossians 3:12-14).

A measure of our true spirituality is the flow of God's love from our lives. The Apostle Paul reminds us that *"God has poured out his love into our hearts by the Holy Spirit, whom he has given us."* (Romans 5:5) This truth is borne out by Jesus Christ because he showed both compassion and tough love when both were called for.

Those who 'Proclaim' the Message of the Scriptures and Witness

There are very important conditions placed on all those who *'proclaim'*, by any method, the truths of the Scriptures, that is, that they do this through the leading and power of God's Holy Spirit, coupled with prayer. This means that they will not depend on their own resources but depend on His. When this does not occur, there can be little or much energy expended with no positive spiritual result. It must always be borne in mind that it's not just *what* is said that is important but *how* it is said, and an essential quality in those who speak for the Lord is winsomeness, that is, a winning attractive and engaging manner.

The important twin factors in proclamation – Obedience and Compassion

The secret of a God approved and Spirit led ministry is *obedience* - not success, failure, achievements, people converted or discipled, but being obedient to that which God lays on the 'proclaimer's' heart. The results are in God's hands, not the one who proclaims.

The following are a few guidelines from the Scriptures:

- "To obey is better than sacrifice" (1 Samuel 15:22).

- Jesus said, "My sheep listen to my voice; I know them, and they follow me." (John 10:27)

- Peter and the other apostles replied, "We must obey God rather than men!" (Acts 5:29)

- This is how we know that we love the children of God: by loving God and carrying out

- His commands" (1 John 5:2).

- Moses had to learn obedience to God beforeHe could be used by Him (Exodus 3).

All Christians are meant to be involved in 'ongoing outreach' to those outside God's Kingdom in everyday life and situations, so they must not only learn to listen and obey, but do so with compassion as Jesus Christ did.

Preaching the Whole Gospel

Preachers are not at liberty to preach a partial Gospel, but only the 'whole' Gospel, the whole counsel of God as outlined in the following Scriptures: Acts 20:20; & 25-27, Romans 15:14-19, 1 Corinthians 2:4-5, 2 Corinthians 12:12, Colossians 1:25-29 & 2 Timothy 4:17.

Note also, the warning given in Ezekiel 3:15-21, and the conviction of Paul in 1 Corinthians 9:16.

It is also very important to understand that those who preach or proclaim the Gospel in various ways as outlined below, should always be aware that to be effective for God they must be the channel through whom His Holy Spirit can flow in power. This means that they must remain a pure channel.

The Power of True Christian Proclamation

A word of testimony is a powerful way to witness to people, because it involves the sharing of personal experience, and our words become endued with the power of God when it is expressed with sincerity and humility. (Matthew 10:32-33)

Is your name in the Book?

Christians need to know, and have confidence, that their salvation in Christ is assured, and that their *"... names are written in the book of life"* (Philippians 4:3 & Daniel 12:1).

Illustration for the Gospel

An Old violin up for auction for just a few pounds is bought by a skilled violinist. He takes the battered old violin, cleans and adjusts it, and he plays it beautifully. Its price is now very high. Application: We may consider our lives are not worth much (low self-worth), until given to the Master, who takes the battered old life, cleans and adjusts it so that it becomes a life that produces 'a fine melody' of high worth all through the Master hand of Jesus.

When preaching the Good News, the Gospel, there should be a balance of saying what we are saved *from,* and what we are saved *to.*

It is well to note the approach that Jesus used in

reaching out to the woman of Samaria whom He met at a well. He introduced himself as the Messiah because he loves to take the *lost*, the *last*, the *least* and the *lowest* and make something beautiful of them. God's love to the lost is *not* based on looks, personality, wealth, or even moral goodness, it is offered without any preconditions and it is undeserved – it's God's grace.

With reference to saving and losing our lives for Christ, (Matthew 16:25) Those who share the Gospel with others must also share their lives (1 Thessalonians 2:8). The effectiveness of a person's ministry depends on the fervency of their Love for God and others.

A Call to Lead

Commission

There are those who are directly called by God for service in God's Kingdom, and others who are called by men to fill positions of responsibility as set out in the Scriptures for service in God's kingdom. In each case they should be especially appointed (anointed by God) for this service. They may experience this through a strong and constant burden to lead others to Christ and disciple them.

Essential qualities in a Leader:

- their lifestyle as seen by their faith in God –
  see Hebrews 13:7 & 17

- a servant heart – see Matthew 20:25-28

- God's power manifesting in their speech –
  see 1 Corinthians 2:4-5

- speech which is true to the Scriptures and in
  context – see 2 Timothy 2:15

- the ability to remind others that all Scripture
  is God-breathed and the necessity to
  converse with the Living God – see 2 Timothy
  3:16; 1 Timothy 3:15; & 1 Timothy 4:7-10

- the ability to inspire others to follow them –
  see Mark 1:17-18

God warns those who speak in his name but whose prophecies are false, that they will perish.

God informs Jeremiah that they are telling lies; and that He had not sent them, appointed them, or spoken to them. (Jeremiah 14:14-15)

Those commissioned by God

It is interesting to note that many of those called directly by God were reluctant to accept the calling and their responses ranged from an inability to speak well, inadequacy and fear, to being overly confident. However, as they submitted themselves to God and learned to put their trust in Him and not themselves, they proved God was able to achieve His purposes through them. Listed below are some names of people in the Bible who were called directly by God:

Abraham - Genesis 12:1-3

Moses - Exodus 3:1-10, 1 Samuel 12:6

David - 1 Samuel 16:1 & 11-13, 1 Samuel 13:14

Jeremiah - Jeremiah 1:4-8

Daniel - Daniel 5:11-12

Jonah - Jonah 1:1-3

The Lord Jesus Christ - Matthew 1:18-23, 3:11-17, Luke 1:26-56 Jesus' was a unique 'calling' and He had no character defects.

Jesus' Disciples - Matthew 10:1-4, Mark 3:14-19, Luke 10:1, John 15:16

John the Baptist - Luke 1:11-20 & 57-66

The Apostle Paul - Acts 9:11-19, 13:2, 1 Timothy 1:12-14, 2:7, 2 Timothy 1:11

Apostles, Prophets, Evangelists, Pastors, Teachers – 1 Corinthians 12:6-8, & 27-31, 1 Corinthians 14:1-5, Ephesians 4:11-13

Those who serve, encourage, contribute to the needs of others – Romans 12:6-8

Those given spiritual gifts of wisdom, knowledge, faith, healing, miraculous powers, prophecy, discernment between spirits, speaking in tongues, administration - 1 Corinthians 12:4-11, & 27-31, 1 Corinthians 13:1-3, Hebrews 13:7 & 17.

Any perceived 'call' from God needs to be carefully weighed, as very few people receive a calling into service of some kind as clearly as Moses did (Exodus 3:1-10), Samuel (1 Samuel 3:1-19), Jeremiah (Jeremiah 1:5), the Disciples (Matthew 4:18-22, Mark 2:13-14, John 1:35-51), or the Apostle Paul (Acts 9:1-20).

It is a more common experience for those called to carry a burden, or conviction in their hearts. This may occur, however, only after repeated 'calls' in various ways, perhaps, due to the fact that we are often 'dull' at hearing or interpreting the voice of God.

Those commissioned by men

The men that carry out this function are led by the Holy Spirit to recognise those to be commissioned. For example, the Apostles and the elders made a decision on the basis that *"it seemed good to us and the Holy Spirit"* (Acts 15:22, 28). This forms a good guiding principle when Church leaders or other decisions concerning believers are to be made.

This process of recognition of leaders is enacted by the 'laying on of hands', as seen in the following Scripture:

> *"So after they had fasted and prayed, they placed their hands on them and sent them off."*[5]

> *(Acts 13:3)*

There are two specific church leadership positions recognised in the N.T. namely, elder and deacon.

Elder

Paul and Barnabas appointed elders in each church (Acts 14:2), and the qualities stated for Elder are given below:

> *"He must be above reproach, the husband of but one wife, temperate, self-controlled, respectable, hospitable, able to teach, not*

given to drunkenness, not violent but gentle, not quarrelsome, not a lover of money. He must manage his own family well and see that his children obey him with proper respect. (If anyone does not know how to manage his own family, how can he take care of God's church?). He must not be a recent convert, or he may become conceited and fall under the same judgement as the devil. He must also have a good reputation with outsiders, so that he will not fall into disgrace and into the devil's trap." [6]

(1 Timothy 3:1-7)

Deacon

Deacons, likewise, are to be men worthy of respect, sincere, not indulging in much wine, and not pursuing dishonest gain. They must keep hold of the deep truths of the faith with a clear conscience. They must first be tested; and then if there is nothing against them, let them serve as deacons. In the same way, their wives are to be women worthy of respect, not malicious talkers but temperate and trustworthy in everything. A deacon must be the husband of but one wife and must manage his children and his household well. Those who have served well gain an excellent standing and great assurance in their faith in Christ Jesus. (1 Timothy 3:8-13, Acts 6:1-10).

The qualifications for elders and deacons are more to do with character than formal scholarly qualifications, positions in society or through lineage. Elders and deacons are expected to use their appointed authority with love, humility, diligence and discipline as embodied in the Scriptures given above.

We read in 1 Timothy 3:1-2, 5:17 show that an elder's responsibilities were: to teach and preach, and direct the affairs of the church. Also, he was to shepherd the flock of God, and guard the Church from error. (Acts 20:28-31)

It is clearly implied in the above Scriptures that elders should have a close relationship with God, know the Scriptures and how to apply them to themselves, their family and to the members of their congregation. Their remit of authority only extends to the people in their congregation, and only concerns their spiritual health, growth and lifestyle, and is not to be used in an overbearing or controlling fashion. The whole Church operates by consent with the people in the congregation being prepared to submit to the authority of the elders in matters of biblical teaching and spiritual direction.

In the N.T. it shows is clear that elders were appointed in each Church, and not an elder, but elders,[7] and this plurality of leadership provides an added safeguard against erroneous teaching and confirmation of spiritual direction.

Service

Before considering the type of service we should be involved in as Christians, it is wise to first pay attention to making some progress at *being* the person God wants us to *be*, in terms of addressing basic un-Christlike character defects, and then, to concentrate on *doing* what we sense God is calling us to *do*.

The being aspect referred to is seen in the attitude the person has towards those they are seeking to serve, and the task to be done. Also, when we are considering whether to undertake any Christian service, we should carefully assess our gifting for that type of service. In a rarer case it may be God calls some of us to a field of service that we do not feel particularly suited to, and it becomes a faith and trust issue for us.

The qualities which are most important are a servant heart, a right motive, humility, faith, love, grace followed by the use of the ability God has given. Jesus Christ, above all others, showed us the best example of a true servant. We are told that:

> *"Our attitude should be the same as that of*
> *Christ Jesus who, being in very nature God,*
> *did not consider equality with God*
> *something to be grasped, but made himself*

nothing, taking the very nature of a servant,
being made in human likeness. And being
found in appearance as a man, he humbled
himself and became obedient to death -
even death on a cross!"

The following are some examples of those with a servant heart in the N.T.:

- The Lord Jesus Christ - Acts 3:26; 4:27;

- David – Acts 4:25;

- Christians – Acts 4:29; 2 Timothy 2:24;

- Paul – Romans 1:1; Galatians 1:10; Ephesians 3:7;

- Phoebe – Romans 16:1;

- Tychicus – Ephesians 6:21;

- Epaphras – Colossians 1:7;

Jesus told the parable of the man going on a journey who gave his servants five talents of money, two talents and one talent, and when he returned, he wanted to know what they had done with what they had been given (Matthew 25:14-30). The main lesson from the story is that, it's not what we have, it's what we do with what we have, that really matters.

So, whatever we do, we are expected to step out in faith for God, not looking for the approval of others, but fulfilling God's will for us.

We, as believers, are called to:

- serve Him without fear – Luke 1:74.

- serve only Him – Luke 4:8; 16:13.

- serve Him in humility, remembering that you have nothing "that you did not receive" – 1 Corinthians 4:7; Acts 20:19; Colossians 3:12; 1 Peter 5:5.

- serve constantly, with diligence – Luke 12:37.

- serve Him whole heartedly – Romans 1:9, Ephesians 6:7.

- serve Him through the Holy Spirit, and not through the old way of the written code – Romans 7:6.

- use our freedom to serve one another in love – Galatians 5:13; Matthew 20:26-28.

- serve the living God and not idols – 1

Thessalonians 1:9.

- have our service tested, if we are deacons –
  1 Timothy 3:10.

- use our gifts to serve others, always
  remembering *"I can do everything through
  him who gives me strength"* – Philippians
  4:13; 1 Peter 4:10. Be a holy priesthood
  serving God – 1 Peter 2:5, Revelation 1:5-6.

Hebrews 12:1 exhorts us to, *"throw off everything
that hinders"*, so we are to be careful to identify
God's priorities for our lives, and become familiar
with His purposes and ordained activities. We must
avoid becoming so involved with the work of God,
that we neglect the God of the work.

It should be borne in mind that when we receive a
call to serve God in some way, the task will be
beyond us, and that's on purpose, because he
wants us to learn to be dependent on Him such
that His name will be glorified.

Giving

Our service to God and others will require us to
have a cheerful, giving attitude as shown in 2
Corinthians with a reminder that:

> *"Whoever sows sparingly will also reap*

sparingly, and whoever sows generously will also reap generously. Each man should give what he has decided in his heart to give, not reluctantly or under compulsion, for God loves a cheerful giver."

(2 Corinthians 9:6 from Psalm 112:9)

Verse 10 states that God will supply and increase our store of seed and enlarge our harvest of righteousness. In contrast to this, God gives the warning in Haggai 1:4-9 that a situation may arise where we have planted much, but have harvested little; we eat, but never have enough; we put on clothes, but are not warm; and the theme continues. God explains the reason for this - *"Because of My house, which remains a ruin, while each of you is busy with his own house."*

The only buildings God commissioned was the Tabernacle through Moses, and the Temple built through David and Solomon. God has no physical building now.

A good example of giving is shown in *"... they gave themselves first to the Lord and then to us"*, (2 Corinthians 8:5) indicating that if a person first gives their heart to the Lord there will be no difficulty in giving him anything else. Ultimately God Himself is the best example of sacrificial giving as seen in "God so loved that he gave ..." (John 3:16)

Our Weakness – His Strength

God wants us to use the gifting and talents we have been given, but to always act with humility and be prepared to be led by the Holy Spirit, and so bringing praise to God, not ourselves.

Let us consider the Apostle Paul, the gifted writer of much of the New Testament, who was greatly used to teach and establish many churches, and who was also used by God to effect miraculous healings. To prevent him from becoming conceited, God gave him a "thorn in the flesh" and said:

> *"My grace is sufficient for you, for my power is made perfect in weakness."*
>
> *(2 Corinthians 12:7-10)*

This means that God's ability and authority will work through those believers who admit that they are not able to achieve the spiritual objective of a task or action but are dependent on the Holy Spirit to do that through them or another channel.

For example, Paul could travel to a place and preach and teach, but he would be dependent on the guidance and power of the Holy Spirit to bring conversions to Christ and to cause people to respond positively to the teaching of the Bible.

Leadership

The leadership role is crucial in all spheres of activity, whether secular or religious, and is especially true for the Christian Church. Over the years leadership role models have changed, and it is particularly important for present day Church leaders to note the changes that have occurred from O.T. days to now.

In the O.T. we have the leadership models of Moses, Judges, the Kings and the Prophets where their words were authoritative and final, and covered all areas of judgement and direction from domestic to military affairs. The role and authority of the Prophet as God's spokesman who provides direction and leadership is seen in Deuteronomy 18:15-22. This Scripture also contains a warning to 'false prophets'. When these leaders were obeying God, they were submitting to His Lordship in all matters, but when they followed their own counsel, they were not acknowledging him as Lord.

The Jewish religious leaders of Jesus' day were severely criticised by Jesus (Matthew 23), and were accused by Him of hypocrisy, double standards and for teaching the precepts of men as the commandments of God, and also for failing to teach Scriptural truth.

The line of command of O.T. Kings and up to

present-day governments is long, with officials at each level reporting to those above them right up to the top. However, the line of command for the N.T. Church, and that includes the present-day Church, is short, as it has Christ as its head, and the only two Church offices mentioned in the N.T. are those of elder (also called an overseer) and deacon, and these are only to represent local Churches. To these are added the major offices of apostles, prophets, evangelists, pastors and teachers. (Ephesians 4:11)

The role of Christian leadership in a Church situation is different in some respects to the way in which leadership is carried out in industry and commerce. One of these differences is shown in the exercise and understanding of authority. In a company, authority may be exercised with or without, much concern for the people they manage. However, in a Church there must always be consideration of others, and where people have a different view, the situation must be explained with patience, love and grace. In Christian leadership authority is *given,* not *taken.*

A common difficulty for Church leaders concerns the handling of 'a vision' of a way forward and its practical outworking, and this situation calls for it to be immersed in prayer and handled with humility, explaining with care and clear scriptural principles how the vision is to be fulfilled. Using this approach leaders should be able to take people with them, bearing in mind the adage, 'you are only a leader if others willingly follow you'.

An important aspect of Church leadership is that the leader needs to spend time waiting on the Lord in prayer to 'hear' what He is saying, and so be able to translate God's word, God's vision to the other church members (Jeremiah 23:16-22, Acts 26:19). Further guidance is given on 'vision' as revealed in Habakkuk 2:1-3 where the prophet was asked to wait on God for his appointed timing when the vision should be given – this calls for patience.

In the Scriptures, there are many aspects of leadership that can be taken note of, such as the humility of Moses, and the boldness, courage, faithfulness, suffering and obedience in the O.T. prophets, and some of the Judges and Kings (especially David), and in the N.T. there is the Lord Jesus Christ, the apostles and sometimes Jesus' disciples.

A key hallmark of good, biblical based leadership is humility, as embodied in Moses (Numbers 12:3), who led a nation from captivity in Egypt, through the daunting wilderness to the 'Promised Land'. In that long journey, taking many years, he had many things to learn and that included, accepting his mission and leadership role (ref: Exodus 3&4),

accepting advice from his father-in-law, and how not to assume or act in arrogance, but to follow closely what God said.[8]

The appointment of people to positions of authority within the Church should not be a hasty matter, as confirmed in 1 Timothy 5:22. Also, elders should be:

"Blameless - not overbearing, not quick-tempered, not given to drunkenness, not violent, not pursuing dishonest gain."

(Titus 1:5-9),

and

"... not lording it over those entrusted to you but being examples to the flock."

(1 Peter 5:3)

When spiritual leaders use 'their gifts', they should remember that without Him, they "can do nothing" effective for God.[9]

Those in Church leadership or others who contribute in any way to the edifying or building up of the church such as those who serve, encourage, contribute to the needs of others (Romans 12:6-8); those given spiritual gifts of wisdom, knowledge, faith, healing, miraculous powers, prophecy, discernment between spirits, speaking in tongues, administration (1 Corinthians 12:4-11, & 27-31, 1 Cor inthians 13:1-3), they must bear in mind that whatever spiritual gifts they have been given, are to be used with humility and through the leading of the Holy Spirit.

1 Corinthians 13 expresses the motivation for the use of these gifts - love. When leaders are appointed, they should be aware that they will have trials and difficulties as well as blessings. The difficult times can happen in various ways, either from internal or external factors. Difficult situations can come from our thoughts and actions, but when the leader is in the wrong, they should quickly repent and show their repentance through appropriate actions. When difficulties come from external sources over which they have no influence, then they can feel sorry for themselves or take this as an opportunity to trust God more through the testing time. But wherever the troubles come from, they provide an opportunity for the person to become a more mature Christian.

The potential quality of spiritual leadership in a person is often seen in their characteristics and lifestyle long before it is recognised in some official way. Many of the qualities of a Christian leader can be observed in the following Scriptures: Moses learnt to depend on God to help him speak and teach, (Exodus 4:10-17) Samuel, in fear of Saul, accepted God's guidance and anointed David to be king, (1 Samuel 16:1-13); God told Jeremiah,:

> *"I appointed you as a prophet to the
> nations", and he answered, "I do not know
> how to speak; I am only a child", whereupon
> God told him not to be afraid and touched
> his mouth, enabling him to speak*
>
> *(Jeremiah 1:4-8)*

We also see that leaders are supposed to be gentle with fellow believers, like a mother caring for little children, and they are to not only share the Gospel with them, but their lives as well. (1 Thessalonians 2:7-8) Another factor worth noting about these leaders, is that they don't claim to be competent, but their competence comes from God. (2 Corinthians 3:5-6).

If individuals, however godly in lifestyle, have been appointed to a position of Church leadership and they fail to provide a clear example that others are willingly prepared to follow, then their leadership should be called into question. The other extreme is where the person shows leadership qualities that call people to follow them unquestioningly. This is dangerous form of leadership, and a common feature of Sects. If, on the other hand, the leader leads by example, is sound in the principles of Scripture, is humble, has an attitude of servanthood, is open to question and the 'lead direction' is not for the leader's benefit, but for those that would follow – this then, is an example of good leadership.

Another situation to be wary of is when a person puts themselves forward as a leader without the recognition and confirmation of other mature Christians.

Christian Maturity and Leadership Characteristics

The common goal for those who aspire for Christian maturity or leadership is to seek to become more Christ-like in character. The maturing process, by its very nature, is never very quick and the person has to be prepared to take knocks, be patient, humble, and gracious, always ready to forgive and to seek forgiveness, and fully committed to follow the teaching of Scripture and the Holy Spirit's leading.

As part of the discipleship process, we should listen because we are told that:

> "If you are not disciplined (and everyone undergoes discipline), then you are illegitimate children and not true sons. Moreover, we have all had human fathers who disciplined us and we respected them for it. How much more should we submit to the Father of our spirits and live!"
>
> (Hebrews 12:8-9)

Check your credentials!

So, how do you handle correction? By killing the messenger? By making sure he or she never gets to you again? By keeping score and saying, 'Look what I've accomplished; what have you accomplished?' By giving in to self-pity and saying, 'People do not understand or appreciate me?' Your mind needs to be sharpened constantly, so stay open to those whom God sends to do it.

Those who show signs of maturity would not retaliate when wrongfully accused; have no need to be 'proven right'; stay calm in a crisis; praise others, but not themselves; put the interests of others before their own; show practical love for fellow believers; always seek a closer walk with God, but never consider themselves to *'Have Arrived'*; immediately commit all problems to prayer with thanksgiving. (Philippians 4:6). Also, they should rejoice with those who rejoice, show sensitivity to those going through a tough time, and mourn with those who mourn. (Romans 12:15)

Self-Assessment questions

Are we humble? God says, *"This is the one I esteem: he who is humble and contrite in spirit, and trembles at my word."*[10] (Isaiah 66:2)

Do we have a tendency to be domineering?

The guidelines for the way to treat or handle others, states:

"Do not rebuke an older man harshly, but exhort him as if he were your father. Treat younger men as brothers, older women as mothers, and younger women as sisters, with absolute purity."[11]

(1 Timothy 5:1-2)

Do we always speak the truth in love? (Ephesians 4:15)

The business of speaking the truth in a loving manner can be difficult, but truth and love is a couplet that should never be separated.

So, let us remember that – *"the heart reflects the person"* for example, when Samuel was seeking to select the next king:

"... the LORD said to Samuel, 'Do not consider his appearance or his height, for I have rejected him. The LORD does not look at the things man looks at. Man looks at the outward appearance, but the LORD looks at the heart.'"[12]

(1 Samuel 16:7)

Sanctification
When we recognise our need to be forgiven and

get right with God, we start our new life with vibrancy and joy, but as an immature Christian. At the beginning of this new relationship between God and ourselves, God begins to change our motives and aims in life and our character. God's purpose in all this change is to make us more Christ like in our character, and this process of change is referred to as 'sanctification' and lasts a lifetime.

The amount of character change and spiritual maturity that occurs, however, depends on our response, and whether we recognise our need to go on changing and our ability to learn lessons through the mistakes that they we make in life, and also to learn to trust God through events and experiences over which we have no control.

When Christians fail to learn from their mistakes and experiences, they will be quite immature at the end of their lives and will have forfeited much of the joy and peace that God intended them to have. So, basically it can be said that the process of sanctification begins at the time when we first put our faith in the Lord Jesus Christ alone for forgiveness and salvation, and the process continues throughout life. Guidance for the process of sanctification is given in the following Scripture -

"It is God's will that you should be sanctified: that you should avoid sexual immorality;

that each of you should learn to control his own body in a way that is holy and honourable, not in passionate lust like the heathen, who do not know God; and that in this matter no-one should wrong his brother or take advantage of him. The Lord will punish men for all such sins, as we have already told you and warned you. For God did not call us to be impure, but to live a holy life. Therefore, he who rejects this instruction does not reject man but God, who gives you his Holy Spirit".[13]

(1 Thessalonians 4:3-8)

It helps at all times when we remember to give thanks to the Lord for His unfailing love and wonderful deeds as He satisfies the thirsty and fills the hungry with good things. (Psalms 107:8-9) Also, the word of God is a means by which we become sanctified as confirmed by Jesus' words – "Sanctify them by the truth; your word is truth." (John 17:17). It is important to pursue an ongoing lifestyle of obeying and willingly following God's Word, and that means being prepared to be set apart for God's use. Also, the people referred to in 1 Corinthians 6:11 were far away from God, but He changed them - *"But you were washed, you were sanctified, you were justified in the name of the Lord Jesus Christ and by the Spirit of our God."*

Spirituality

If we seek to follow the leading of the Holy Spirit, but then choose to link ourselves with non-Christians, and get drawn into an unhelpful lifestyle, we will find we get into a state of inner conflict of morals, and risk compromising our Christian values. So, we will have to choose our company with care; when with non-Christians, we can be friendly, but always prepared to speak the truth in a loving manner. Also, when we know we have made a mess of things, we need to be quick to repent, and get right with others. The best way we can steer through the Christian life and minimise the failures and difficulties previously mentioned, is to determine to begin each day by reading His Word, praying and listening, and then seeking to obey what He says.

Supernatural and Sacrificial

The Lord spoke to David and told him to build an altar to the Lord on the threshing-floor of Araunah. David asked him for the site, and Araunah was willing to give it to him, but David would only accept it by paying the full price for it. This illustrates that God's service has the sacrificial element. (1 Chronicles 21:18-24 - 22:1)

On the other hand, if we do God's work relying only on ourselves, our ability, our knowledge, and so on, without spending time in God's presence and in His Word. Then this approach, despite much hard work, will achieve nothing for God. However, by contrast, Paul achieved so much for God through his teaching and preaching and with God's help building up the Church, and writing much of the New Testament, but it cost him much suffering, and he was stoned almost to death. (Acts 14:19)

Practical Holiness

Let us be mindful of the winnowing fork of the Lord Jesus Christ (Matthew 3:11-12) and let us be winsome (attractive of manner, engaging, bright, winning), and also follow what God requires of us as stated in Micah 6:8. A well-known preacher had been spoken about in an untruthful way, and he felt bitter about it. A friend came to see him who, after a brief condolence, said - *"unless you utterly forgive those people, the bitterness and unforgiveness in you will act as a blockage and you will be prevented from going on with God"*. He did forgive, and the weight lifted from his spirit.

Those who came into direct contact with His moral majesty and purity were overwhelmed as is shown for example in the passage Isaiah 6:1-13. Recognition of and submission to His holiness are the divine prerequisites for admission to the inner heart of God and the most important requirements for knowing Him and fulfilling His Will for us, and is also the most important qualification for learning from Him.

> *"Make every effort to live in peace with all men and to be holy; without holiness no-one will see the Lord."*[14]
>
> *(Hebrews 12:14)*

The Priesthood of all Believers

When the Church was first set up there would have been a clear tendency to adopt a secular organisational model, but that was not God's model. His was to be a spiritual model that He would instruct and resource as He so desired. So, whilst the Church was set up with elders and deacons, with their responsibilities, God gave spiritual giftings to whom He chose, and referred to believers as 'a royal priesthood'; hence, He no longer required the role of a priest to act as an intermediary between them and God0 However, now we can connect directly with Jesus the Great High Priest (Hebrews 4:14). Priests today, in formal churches, are ordained church elders.

Given below are extracts of Scriptures that relate to this teaching:

- "you are a chosen people, a royal priesthood, a holy nation," 1 Peter 2:4-10

- "in Christ we who are many form one body,

and each member belongs to all the others."Romans 12:5-8.

- "Now to each one the manifestation of the Spirit is given for the common good." 1 Corinthians 12:7-1;

  - Note that it does not say that spiritual gifts are given to people holding a certain position in the Church.

- This Scripture refers to brothers contributing gifts/words in a service, 1 Corinthians 14:26-40

- "teaching and admonishing one another", Colossians 3:16

- "Confess *your* trespasses to one another, and pray for one another, that you may be healed." James 5:14-16

- Christ "has made us to be a kingdom and priests" Revelation 1:5-6.

According to the term "a royal priesthood" in 1 Peter 2:5-9; the former term is associated with offering spiritual sacrifices, the latter with the royal dignity of showing forth the Lord's excellencies.The apostle Peter pictures the Church as a building constructed of living stones with Christ as the Chief Cornerstone and this represents the congregation as a company of priests of royal lineage with Christ as the great King High Priest when they meet together.

In the above Scriptures, there is a common theme of participation by believers in the congregation making contributions as led by God's Holy Spirit (1 Corinthians 14:26-40), with a caution given in verse 40 that *"everything should be done in a fitting and orderly manner."* This 'order,' however, should be God's order that may not necessarily be ours, so this calls for people being sensitive to the leading of the Holy Spirit.

Practical Illustration

This teaching states that each Christian in a Church has an opportunity to be a participant in a Church service, through choosing hymns/songs, giving a Bible reading, praying, giving a short word of testimony, and using gifts of the Holy Spirit as they sense His leading. This participation should be by general invitation of the church leadership and the extent of its practice will be determined by the church leadership and the size of the congregation.

A caution that needs to apply with this participation is when someone believes they have received a directional or warning word from God, in which case they should share it first with an elder, and the word can then be 'weighed or considered' by the elders, and if they discern it to be a word from the Lord for the congregation, the member should then be allowed to deliver it to the Church.

Submission to God - Overcoming the clash of wills

The very word 'submission' does not sit easily with us because it goes against our natural instincts of wanting to be in control of every aspect of our lives. So, the thought of having to 'submit' to somebody else's will and lead often brings about a clash of wills. However, when God asks us to 'submit' our lives to Him, it becomes easier to do when we know something of the character of God and that He has our best interests at heart. So, whilst the initial act of submission to God may be difficult, once we realise His goodness and grace, we will learn to trust Him more and continue to submit their our lives to Him.

As we consider the whole act of 'submission', let us remember that although God is our Creator, He does not wish to dominate and control us like puppets, but He invites us to submit to Him as a loving Father and become His sons and daughters. When this occurs, we will discover the practical outworking of 'His and our best' for our lives. It should be borne in mind that submission to God is not weakness, but wisdom.

Ongoing Submission – the key to being effective for God

When we overcome the potential clash of wills for the first time and submit to the will of God, this is the point at which we become believers. However, this step of faith initiates an ongoing internal struggle where we will often be tempted to go our own way. This means that for the rest of our Christian journey, we will be faced with situations where we will have to decide whether to submit or not.. It is as this process of ongoing submission continues that the person becomes more and more convinced of God's goodness and graciousness, discovered first and foremost through His demonstration of forgiveness and salvation, and further realised and experienced in all aspects of our lives.

The whole process of submission is always a voluntary action on the part of the believer. This is illustrated by the following scripture:

> *"The mind of sinful man is death, but the mind controlled by the Spirit is life and peace; the sinful mind is hostile to God. It does not submit to God's law, nor can it do so."* [15]

> *(Romans 8:6-7).*

The above is accomplished in practice by the believer being prepared to be led by the Holy Spirit, as was Peter in the following account:

> *"Then Peter, filled with the Holy Spirit, said to them: "Rulers and elders of the people!"*[16]
>
> *(Acts 4:8)*

Submission is closely linked with humility, and He is looking for humility and submission in us, as shown in the Scripture:

> *"God opposes the proud but gives grace to the humble. Submit yourselves, then, to God. Resist the devil, and he will flee from you."*
>
> *(James 4:6-7)*

Living in the *'Will of God'* is fulfilling the *'Word of God'* as it is revealed to you personally and obeying Him as he speaks to you. God has a number of ways in which He 'speaks' to us, including through the following: reading the Bible; biblical preaching; personal and wider circumstances; biblical meditation; inner convictions of the Holy Spirit. The more we submit to God the more closely will be our fellowship with Him and guidance from Him.

Submission and Healing

God can't heal what you won't reveal to him, or cleanse what you won't confess to him. This statement is illustrated by Jesus telling his disciples that they would all fall away because of Him, and Peter replied:

"'Even if all fall away on account of you, I never will.' Jesus answered, 'this very night, before the cock crows, you will disown me three times.'"

(Matthew 26:31-34 & 69-75).

In the latter verses of this Scripture Peter does deny knowing Jesus three times, and then the cock crows.[17]

Submission – Surrender – Self-Discipline

The devil constantly searches for an entry point into our lives, through our thoughts, and the words of others. We need to always be aware that:

"We wrestle not against flesh and blood but against powers, against the rulers of the darkness of this world."

(Ephesians 6:12).

Your enemy, the devil and his demonic agents, will study you to see which doors he can enter to gain access to your life such as your temper, lust, attitudes, moods, background or past hurts. His first goal is to dominate you; his next is to destroy the purposes of God that are meant to be fulfilled through you. Then he can say to God, "He's mine not yours! He'll obey me, not you!" That's what the battle is all about!

But the good news is that Jesus defeated him – and He has given you the power to do it too. Jesus assured us that, *"Behold I give you power...over all the power of the enemy..."* (Luke 10:19) That means the only power the enemy has over you is the power you give him.

Submission to Spiritual Leaders

As believers, we should be prepared to be subject to the spiritual leaders in our own Church, particularly with regard to our lifestyle, that is, as long as the direction and teaching given by the leadership is in line with the principles of Scripture. We are enjoined to,

> *"Remember your leaders, who spoke the word of God to you. Consider the outcome of their way of life and imitate their faith."*
>
> *(Hebrews 13:7)*

If your leader meets this standard, you should obey them as it later states -

> *"Obey your leaders and submit to their authority. They keep watch over you as men who must give an account. Obey them so that their work will be a joy, not a burden, for that would be of no advantage to you."*
>
> *(Hebrews 13:17)*

Believers in a congregation should not be subjected

to any form of 'heavy shepherding' that is, where leaders want you to obey them without questioning. Rather, leaders should have the characteristics and lifestyle of those who rely on the Lord for wisdom and patience, having a good knowledge of the Scriptures and Biblical principles, coupled with love, grace, humility, a strong resolve, spiritual insight and boldness of faith. It follows, therefore, that if these qualities of leadership exist, then there would be no need to resort to any type of heavy guidance.

Submission to Others

The Scriptures state that believers should also *"submit to one another"* (Ephesians 5:21) and be *"competent to instruct one another"* (Romans 15:14). These aspects of the believers' life should develop through relationships and proven trust over time.[18]

We are also asked to submit ourselves to the governing authorities; , where it states:

> *"Submit yourselves for the Lord's sake to every authority instituted among men: whether to the king, as the supreme authority, or to governors, who are sent by him to punish those who do wrong and to commend those who do right."*
>
> *(1 Peter 2:13-14)*

However, there is a guiding principle given by Peter

and John where they questioned the religious authorities who contradict God's Word:

> *"Judge for yourselves whether it is right in God's sight to obey you rather than God."*
>
> (Acts 4:13-19)

Faith

People use faith/trust every day when they take a ride on a train, for example, they put their faith in the driver to take them safely to their destination. They do not know or see the driver, but they trust him. This analogy can be made when we take an initial step of faith in Christ, and are invited to put our faith in Him for forgiveness and a new start in life with eternal life as our destination.

After we take this initial step of faith, we receive within ourselves a confirmation and inner witness that we have entered into a relationship with God. From this initial step, we are expected to continue to place our faith in Him throughout life, and so develop an increasingly intimate relationship with Him. It follows that what God fundamentally requires of us is to have faith and trust in Him, for the Scripture states:

> *"And without faith it is impossible to please God, because anyone who comes to him must believe that he exists and that he*

rewards those who earnestly seek him."

(Hebrews 11:6)

This confirms the absolute necessity for faith in the Lord Jesus Christ as God if our lives are going to count for Him.

The whole of chapter eleven of the Book of Hebrews is particularly significant on this subject of faith as verse one provides a definition for it and the following verses give us a list of heroes of faith in the pre-Christian era. These verses present us with demonstrations of, and exhortations to, faith. Abraham demonstrated complete faith in God and total availability to him when he said to God, *"Here I am"* (Genesis 22:1), and he showed that he meant it by being prepared to offer up his only son to God as a sacrifice. (Genesis 22:1-19)

Walk of Faith

Faith and fear are enemies – when one is embraced the other retreats. As we exercise faith, it grows. Also, faith is a very close relative of expectation, it's what we believe, not what we feel.

The world says, *"seeing is believing"* but the Christian concept is *"believing is seeing"* –seeing the true character, worth, love, grace, power, and works of God in the Lord Jesus Christ. The barriers to an active faith in the Lord Jesus Christ will include unbelief, ignorance, sin, unforgiveness,

211

bitterness and anger.

The size of our faith determines the outcome of a situation, so to get the right result as far as God is concerned requires belief, determination and the leading of the Holy Spirit. (Isaiah 41:10) God called the Nation of Israel to a life of faith, *"do not fear, for I am with you; do not be dismayed, for I am your God."* It should be noted that there are a number of times in the Bible when people are instructed to *"fear not"*, and this is to encourage us. Let us remember, it is fear that opens the door for the enemy to attack us. We always face a choice of where we invest our faith - whether in the word of man, or the Word of God.

Supernatural Faith

The unique characteristic about the Christian Faith is that it is concerned with people having a living trusting relationship with the One True and Only God who operates supernaturally, often on His own, and at times through people, especially through those who have chosen to follow Him. However, as we look at the history of the Church, we can see from its many shortcomings that too often Christians are not living close enough to God to hear what He is saying and lack the utter dependency required, coupled with the necessary obedience to provide the evidence for a 'supernatural' faith. The following Scripture illustrates this type of faith:

> *"I came to you in weakness and fear, and with much trembling. My message and my preaching were not with wise and persuasive words, but with a demonstration of the Spirit's power, so that your faith might not rest on men's wisdom, but on God's power."*
>
> *(1 Corinthians 2:3-5)*

This Scripture typically portrays Paul as having the necessary characteristics for this type of faith. Hence, it can be seen from this Scripture that those who have faith in God are not trusting in their own ability or strength to live the Christian life, but they are trusting in God's power.

Assurance

Assurance is gained through living a life trusting God, accepting the guidance of God's Holy Spirit and obeying the Bible. As we continue to live in this way, our confidence grows as we see more of His wisdom, and understand and experience more of His goodness, grace and love. All this experience in life provides the foundation for being assured of things that we have not yet experienced such as eternal life and heaven.

Let us remember that as Christians, we are called to persevere to the end:

"All men will hate you because of me, but he who stands firm to the end will be saved." [19]

(Matthew 10:22)

Having 'assurance' is an integral part of our faith in Christ, and is shown by a confidence that we show in our attitudes and actions, and how we demonstrate the outworking of that faith in a positive manner in our daily lives. When this confidence is lacking, we experience doubts, which can have serious consequences such as the following:

- we put limits on what God can do - Matthew 14:31, 21:21

- we lose direction in their life - Luke 24:38

- we become uncertain of what to do - Romans 14:23

- we experience a loss of blessings and benefits from God - James 1:6

Nevertheless, we should have compassion and be merciful to those who doubt. (Jude 1:22)

Prayer

A basic definition of prayer would be that 'Prayer is communication with God'. Prayer may be defined in its most basic sense as communication with God.

God always wants us to communicate with Him –
whether we feel like it or not. This involves talking
and listening to Him, knowing that He is the living
God (1 Timothy 4:9-10).

A depressing or discouraging situation, or one of
great difficulty may cause us to worry rather than
pray. One place to look for encouragement is to
read the biblical book of Psalms. It is here that we
find writers like David and others express freely
how they feel towards God – their anger,
frustration, trouble – they pour it all out. They ask
for His help and understanding and thank and
praise Him that they can trust Him. It is in prayer
that people make commitments or requests to Him
and He is always listening. One way or another He
provides an answer, unless the person is insincere
or has a wrong motive or attitude. It is always to be
remembered that God reads people's hearts rather
than their lips. Prayer for direction, fellowship, and
seeking His presence, whilst a duty and a discipline,
should also be a delight. A practical approach to
prayer is given in James where people are asked to
pray for the sick, and the person who prays should
pray in faith anointing the sick person with oil. But
it goes on to say that we should *"confess [our] sins
to each other and pray for each other so that [we]
may be healed."* (James 5:14-16)

Prayer Conditions Jesus told the apostles that

when two agreed regarding a matter, it would be done by God (Matthew 18:19). To pray *"in Jesus' name"* means to identify with His character and purposes (John 14:13- 14; 15:16 & 16:23). Also, *"those who seek, knock, and ask receive what they request"* (Matthew 7:7-11). The trust that we have in God, which calms our doubts and uncertainties, also testifies to us that God's answer will come. As we obey the Lord, we are assured that we live in a relationship with Him in which our prayers are heard and answered. (1 John 3:21-22) Matthew 6 reveals 'The Lord's Prayer' that Jesus taught His disciples. It is in two basic parts:

- Declaration to God – v. 9-10.

- Dependency of man – v.11-13.

Prayer Defined

The hymn below, written on the topic of prayer by J. Montgomery (1771-1854) illustrates the essential characteristics of this subject:

1 Prayer is the soul's sincere desire,
Uttered or unexpressed,
The motion of a hidden fire,
That trembles in the breast.

2 Prayer is the burden of a sigh,
The falling of a tear,

The upward glancing of an eye,
When none but God is near.

3 Prayer is the simplest form of speech,
That infant lips can try;
Prayer, the sublimest strains that reach,
The Majesty on high

4 Prayer is the Christian's vital breath,
The Christian's native air,
His watchword at the gate of death;
He enters heaven with prayer.

5 Prayer is the contrite sinner's voice,
Returning from his ways;
While angels in their songs rejoice,
And cry, "Behold, he prays!"

6 O Thou by whom we come to God,
The Life, the Truth, the Way!
The path of prayer Thyself hast trod;
Lord, teach us how to pray.

Prayer as Work

Prayer is more an activity of the spirit than of the mind. May the Lord *"teach us to pray"* (Luke 11:1-4) It is the spiritual, interactive connection that a person has with God that counts when praying, not the many repeated phrases without that vital connection. Jesus reminds us:

"... when you pray, do not keep on babbling like pagans, for they think they will be heard because of their many words."

(Matthew 6:7, & Isaiah 1:15)

Waiting does not come easily to us. In Psalm 40 it states, *"I waited patiently for the LORD; he turned to me and heard my cry."* We need to pray – not for the work, but prayer is the work (Psalm 27:7-8). We need to work heartily (Colossians 3:23) but avoid becoming so involved with the work of God, that we neglect the God of the work (Matthew 11:28-30). We need to pray specifically – not for what He can, but what you believe He will do. Jesus told His disciples that they should always pray and not give up (Luke 18:1-8). This emphasises that persistence is required in prayer.

Prayer that is Heard and Received by God

An example of such a prayer is given in Nehemiah 9:6-15, & 32-38. This prayer was focused on God, reminded Him of His faithfulness to them, was thankful, was repentant in attitude and grounded in Scripture. In Luke 11 Jesus' disciples asked him, *"Lord teach us to pray"* and he responded by sharing the words of the prayer known as 'The Lord's Prayer' (Matthew 6:9-15 & Luke 11:1-4). Prayer should follow this pattern and have the characteristics of being passionate, scriptural, intimate, unhurried, faith-filled and Spirit led.

(Ephesians 6:18, 1 Thessalonians 5:19, & Jude 20). Sometimes prayer will be accompanied by fasting (Matthew 6:16-18). Urgent prayer is characterised by intensive, impassioned crying out to God for help (Matthew 27:46, Luke 18:7-8 & Romans 8:15).

David's prayer in Psalm 55 gives us an example of a person telling God how he feels and makes his requests along with passionate expressions of grief. This type of prayer can be a model for us, it shows us the power of lament as we can mourn personal loss, or the loss of integrity, truth, righteousness and love as we cry out to God to act and change these situations.

So, how should we pray when we are in difficult circumstances? Perhaps a helpful framework for prayer should be along the following lines:

- Tell God how we feel;

- Admit we do not understand the situation;

- Confess any failures or sin on our part;

- Seek the mercy and grace of God for these circumstances;

- Seek God's guidance – continually re-assert, even through tears, our trust in God.

When Christians pray, they should always remember that it is not just 'asking', but every request should always be accompanied by thanksgiving (Philippians 4:6-7), and other Scriptures would add to that praise. Also, powerful and effective prayer should be preceded by confession of sin before God and be entirely reliant on his imputed righteousness (James 5:16). As God knows what's in our hearts, it follows that He will listen more to the inner desire of our hearts, than to the outer expression of our words. (Isaiah 29:13, Mark 7:5-7). We are invited to take all our concerns to God in prayer coupled with thanksgiving, leave them with Him, and then experience His peace in our hearts and minds (Philippians 4:6-7).

Prayer for Healing

In the area of praying for healing there has been much confusion and disappointment, and a way to minimise these effects is to spend time waiting on God in prayer to discover His will in these matters so that we can then pray in accordance with His will, and not ours.

Daily Quiet Time with God

> ... Find a quiet place and choose a time when you will not be interrupted, such as early morning.

... Allow a minimum of twenty minutes if you can.

... Consider some aspects of God's character, confess sin, and worship/praise Him.

... Read the Bible – perhaps a set portion, but most importantly Listen for God to speak, and if you are not 'spoken to' in this portion then keep on reading until you are. You may find Scripture notes helpful.

... Respond to God – *"If you had responded to My rebuke, I would have poured out my heart to you and made my thoughts known to you."* (Proverbs 1:23) It may be a challenge to faith or trust. "We know that God does not listen to sinners. He listens to the godly man who does his will." (John 9:31)

... Record the response, biblical reference and date in a notebook.

... Pray for the people within your sphere of influence, and others the Lord lays on your heart.

... Thank Him for His love and grace.

... The biblical conditions for receiving answers to prayer include trusting God, loving God, freely acknowledging His name, forgiving others, and putting wrong relationships right (Psalm 91:9-16, Matthew 6:15, 1 Peter 3:7-12).

Prayer of St Francis of Assisi 1181-1220

Lord make me a channel of your peace,
that where there is hatred, I may bring love,
where there is discord, I may bring harmony,
where there is doubt, I may bring faith,
where there is despair, I may bring hope,
where there is sadness, I may bring joy.

In this prayer there is clear guidance on how to live as a Christian. An additional aspect would be a reminder *"to speak the truth in a loving way"* (Ephesians 4:15) when we are in a difficult, testing situation.

Introduction to Spirits and Satan

To many people, Satan, demons and evil spirits are the subject of myths, legends or fantasy. There are, however, many references to these terms used in most, if not all, religions.

Also, people are commonly described as having a buoyant spirit; being spirited; a human being is described as consisting of body, mind and spirit. Indeed, a key factor that makes a huge difference between people is the amount of driving force, determination, energy, ambition, and a whole range of character features that define the type of spirit a person possesses.

So, it can be seen that the type of non-physical 'spirit' people possess is the element that best describes their character and is the fundamental initiator that drives them to fulfil their desired actions.

As people are thus led by the spirit element within them, it means that they are sensitive to, and could be influenced by, 'other spirits' around them – the spirits that emanate from the personalities of other people and from other spirits, both good and evil. The good Spirit comes from the good God – the Lord Jesus Christ, and the evil spirits come from the Devil (Satan) and his agents (demons).

Satan

His origin is revealed as a high heavenly being who endeavoured to rise above God his Creator, and was *"cast down to the earth"* (Isaiah 14:12-15). This event is also referred to in (Revelation 12:7-9) where it is recorded that Satan will be hurled to earth, but with his 'angels'– to be known then as demons. Jesus sent out his followers and they reported back that even demons submitted to them, thus demonstrating that Jesus had given them authority over demonic spirits. However, Jesus said to them not to rejoice at this, but rejoice that their names are written in heaven (Luke 10:17-20). This means that Christians have that same authority today over demons, when it is exercised in the name of Jesus.

He is aware of all the work being done that glorifies Jesus, and opposes it, and uses many ways to seek to disrupt, delay or destroy it, and that includes disguising himself as an angel of light (2 Corinthians 11:14), and this can be through well-intentioned people who are not being led by the Holy Spirit. He is a liar, so people not following Jesus closely can be deceived. But he can, and must be resisted (1 Peter 5:8-9, James 4:7). His end is clearly given in Revelation 20:10.

Demons

Their characteristics:

- They are spirits - Matthew 12:43-45;

- They are Satan's emissaries - Matthew 12:26;

- They are numerous - Mark 5:9;

- They can enter into and control men and animals - Mark 5:13, Acts 16:16;

- They can cause mental problems - Mark 5:4-5;

- They can afflict the sick - Matthew 12:22, 210 211 17:15, Luke 13:11-16;

- They are unclean - Matthew 10:1, 12:43;

- They have an eternal destiny - Matthew 25:41;

- They know their end - Matthew 8:29, Luke 8:31;

- They appear religious at times - 1 Timothy 4:1;

- They know Jesus and recognise His authority - Matthew 8:29, James 2:19;

- They are all subject to Jesus - Matthew 4:24, 8:16, 9:32-33, 12:22; • They were cast out by early Christians - Acts 8:7, 16:16;

- They are also subject to Christians today Mark 16:17, Luke 10:17, Acts 16:18, 19:12, 1 John 4:4

Spiritual Warfare

When people become believers in the Lord Jesus Christ and trust in Him as their only and all-sufficient God for their personal salvation, they soon find out that they have entered into an area of spiritual warfare. The reason for having been put into a war zone is the fact that Satan knows he has lost them to God, his sworn enemy, and so he will seek every opportunity to make life difcult for them and try to cause them to disobey God by any means possible.

This warfare shows itself in a variety of ways, direct or subtle, through conflicts in the mind concerning moral standards; relationship difficulties; adverse or challenging circumstances; physical suffering; personal opposition to your views; lifestyle challenges; feeling weak in the face of temptations; find it difficult to pray; doubts concerning the security of our salvation.

There are some positive, but challenging, aspects of suffering for the Christian Faith given in Romans 5:3-5 - it produces, perseverance, which in turn produces character and hope. So, it can be said that it is the pressure of suffering that produces these qualities that otherwise may not have been produced. In view of the above set of difficulties, we need to assess our own personal situation and lifestyle, and as we do this let us remember that God is on our side and we are not let alone or without help.

We can see from the following Scriptures our position of power and authority, and who is against us:

Jesus gave His disciples *"power and authority to drive out all demons and to cure diseases,"* (Luke 9:1). Later, in the times of the Early Church we read how the apostle Paul used the spiritual authority he had been given to cast demons out of a soothsaying girl (Acts 16:18). Paul, writing under the influence of the Holy Spirit stated:

> *"... for though we live in the world, we do not wage war as the world does. The weapons we fight with are not the weapons of the world. On the contrary, they have divine power to demolish strongholds."*
>
> *(2 Corinthians 10:3-5)*

Every controlling habit that does not please God is a demonic stronghold.

In 1 Peter 5:8-9 we are called to be self-controlled and alert because our enemy the devil prowls around like a roaring lion seeking for someone to devour, and we are told to resist him, and stand firm in the faith. It should be remembered that Satan (the devil) has many agents, known as demons. With this in mind, there is a warning given in 1 Corinthians 10:19-21 that sacrifice and worship given to any god or idol, except to the one true and living God, is in fact being offered to demons, and this invites the entrance of demons into the locality. One result from this is that it is much harder to pray, so their presence should be prayed against in the name of Jesus.

In the spiritual battle all Christians are involved in, help is at hand from God, as stated in Philippians 4:19. However, 2 Corinthians 9:10 indicates that our needs are met on a daily basis, just as we pray for our daily bread because bread has a short life span. This keeps people dependent on Him. In Ephesians 6 Paul states clearly the realm of the conflict that every believer is involved in:

"For our struggle is not against flesh and blood, but against the rulers, against the authorities, against the powers of this dark world and against the spiritual forces of evil in the heavenly realms."

(Ephesians 6:10-12)

He then continues by urging us to *"put on the full (whole) armour of God,"* so that when, not if, evil times come, we will be able to stand our ground. He then describes the 'armour' that we need to protect us as:

- The belt of truth

  … we should walk and live in biblical truth because the 'belt' acts as the foundation for holding the other parts of the 'armour' together;

- The breastplate of righteousness

... this piece of armour made of metal plates, covers the front of the body and heart, and refers to our imputed righteous character that protects us from Satan's attacks whilst we are trusting in Christ. (2 Corinthians 5:21)

- Feet fitted with readiness

  ... we should make our journey, always prepared to live and share the gospel of peace;

- The shield of faith

  ... we live in enemy territory, so we can expect 'darts' of temptation, doubt, and disappointments that Satan will shoot at us, so we will need our faith in the Lord Jesus Christ, which acts as a shield to protect us from being hurt or discouraged;

- The helmet of salvation

  ... let us remember, that we are in a spiritual battle, and Satan will suggest thoughts, lies and motives to us, so we will need the helmet of our mind to be protected by God;

- The sword of the Spirit

... the sword is an offensive weapon. This sword is described further as follows:

"For the word of God is living and active. Sharper than any double-edged sword, it penetrates even to dividing soul and spirit, joints and marrow; it judges the thoughts and attitudes of the heart."

(Hebrews 4:12)

Hence, we use it to oppose and disprove Satan's suggestions and temptations, by using Scripture to claim victory in these situations as we are led by the Holy Spirit. So, we need to have a good knowledge of Scripture to recall it when required.

We are also encouraged to *"pray in the Spirit - on all occasions"*, but we need to remember to rely on His Holy Spirit to lead us, thus showing our dependency on Him. This is what it means to *"pray in the Holy Spirit"* (Jude 1:20). It is worth considering, that some of our prayers could be ineffective because we have not first sought the leading of the Holy Spirit before we pray.

Biblical Meditation

Biblical meditation should not be confused with other types of 'meditation' as practised by other religions, because these practices can place people under some form of possession, oppression or dominance by the 'spirits' associated with those religions. When this occurs, the person is not fully responsible for their own actions because they are being influenced to take actions which were not originally their idea. It follows that as they subject themselves to more and more of these 'influences', they run the risk of becoming 'possessed' and under the dominance of these spirits. This in turn can lead to a person suffering from various mental illnesses.

On the other hand, these meditation practices are portrayed as being helpful to people in a whole variety of ways, and many of those who advocate them are not aware of their associated dangers. The good news is that, if the above problems occur, people can be offered special deliverance ministry. By contrast, biblical meditation has only positive outcomes and relates to a person quietly and thoughtfully reading the Bible, considering the message it presents to them, and then praying to God and responding to the message received.

To really hear from God, we need silence as we read His Word and wait for His response to our thoughts on that passage of Scripture, as it is the Holy Spirit who interprets His word, which will lead us to pray in accordance with His will. This process will require time and practice to become more effective at hearing His voice.

Mutual Forgiveness

One of the greatest hindrances to the work of God within the life of a Christian is pride, and it comes in many guises, such as the attitude of holding to the fact that you are right and others are wrong. This means that, even if you are right, the attitude adopted would have helped to destroy any relationship you had with the other person.

Another attitude that is destructive to relationships is refusing to forgive others, even if they have apologised and meant it. When this occurs, we not only hurt the other person, but hinder our own spirit, and from this point onward, we stop the process of maturing further into the person God wants us to be. By contrast, when we truly forgive, then we will experience relief, peace of mind and ongoing blessing from God.

In the Scriptures there is a common theme of forgiveness from God, who requires all people to repent in word, attitude and action. Under the new covenant, we can personally ask for forgiveness on the basis that when the Lord Jesus Christ died on the cross, he died to pay the penalty for the sin of the world including ours. Nevertheless, we each need to repent and thank Him for dying for us personally. When we have taken this step, we should begin to have a more tolerant and forgiving view of those who sin against us.

We are exhorted by God to forgive others - *"Forgive as the Lord forgave you"* (Colossians 3:13) with the condition that, unless we forgive others, He will not forgive us. (Matthew 6:14-15)

We should also note that no exceptions are made. If an exception could have been made for anyone, it would have been Jesus Christ, but he showed us that even when he was being crucified his inherent character was to forgive, and in this extreme situation he said, *"Father, forgive them, for they do not know what they are doing."* (Luke 23:34) We can see, therefore, that God is not asking us to do something that He was not willing to do Himself. Indeed, His was the greatest test of character having been wrongfully accused and put to death.

If we are not willing to forgive others, then apart from the serious consequences mentioned above, there are many other effects that can result as mentioned below:

- blessings withheld from God;

- loss of hearing God's voice;

- loss of spiritual fervour;

- breakdown of relationships;

- loss of support to and from others;

- exclusion/separation through pride of spirit;

- failure to experience release, freedom and a fresh start in life;

- suffering from depression;

- cast a depressive atmosphere around yourself, affecting others;

- others suffer as they know they are not forgiven or accepted.

The dangers of the above effects usually increase with the passage of time, unless the issue is resolved. But God wants us to enjoy freedom from the oppressive and disheartening situations above, and this is gained through forgiving others and thereby knowing His forgiveness and all the blessings which come with it.

Forgiveness

A key aspect in the process of forgiveness is related to the attitude we adopt in judging others. So, when there is a problem with a person, let us approach it with prayer, grace and humility, remembering that the Lord wants us to create an atmosphere not based on judgements but on the anticipation of healing.

Unity – With God and one another

When there is a sense of oneness of purpose and cooperation, much progress is made and people are mutually helped and encouraged. Attitudes that destroy unity are the lack of honesty, humility, and love. Another unhelpful attitude is that of obstinate pride.

All the above unhelpful and counterproductive attitudes may exist not only between people, but also between each Christian and God.

Now let us consider some of the many aspects of unity that God requires Christians to observe and heed, as listed below. He desires us to be united:

- in Christ – Romans 6:5, Philippians 2:1.

- in the worship of God the Father and the Lord Jesus Christ – Matthew 15:9, Luke 4:8, John 4:23 - 24, 1 Timothy 3:15, Hebrews 12:28.

- in the Holy Spirit – Ephesians 4:3.

- in Biblical Truth – Psalms 25:5, 26:3, John 1:17, 14:6, 16:13, Romans 2:8, Ephesians 1:13, 4:14-15, 2 Thessalonians 2:10-12, 1 Timothy 4:16, Titus 1:9.

- in faith and knowledge – Ephesians 4:13.

- in purpose – Psalms 133:1-3, Ephesians 4:2.

- in love for one another – Colossians 1:5, 2:2, 3:14, 1 Peter 1:22.

- in mind, thought and deed – 2 Chronicles 30:12 1 Corinthians 1:10, 1 John 3:18.

- in prayer – Matthew 6:5:13, Acts 4:24, 12:12-17, James 5:14.

- in marriage – Matthew 19:5, Ephesians 5:31, 1 Timothy 4:3.

- in Holy Communion – 1 Corinthians 11:23-29.

The Lord wants His Church to have unity in variety, not unity in conformity. For example, the apostle Paul enjoins:

> *"And over all these virtues put on love, which binds them all together in perfect unity. Let the peace of Christ rule in your hearts, since as members of one body you were called to peace. And be thankful. Let the word of Christ dwell in you richly as you teach and admonish one another with all wisdom, and as you sing psalms, hymns and spiritual*

*songs with gratitude in your hearts to God.
And whatever you do, whether in word or
deed, do it all in the name of the Lord Jesus,
giving thanks to God the Father through
him."* [20]

(Colossians 3:14-17)

One of the reasons why many of the ecumenical movements of our day seemingly achieve little in their efforts to bring about unity is because they are based on compromise, and give rise to the question of which gods are true, and where is the proof? With the Christian Faith there is much proof of Jesus Christ as God. Unity is not something that can be imposed upon the Church by simply getting together; unity needs to be based on Scripture, with views expressed with love, honesty and submission. Therefore, Christians are encouraged as follows:

*"Finally, all of you, live in harmony with one
another; be sympathetic, love as brothers,
be compassionate and humble."* [21]

(1 Peter 3:8)

When Christians are united, they are like Roman soldiers who locked their shields together providing extra protection against the enemy's arrows- like Christians united against the 'arrows' of lies, deceit, unchristian principles and actions. This is helpful, because in Ephesians 6:16 believers

237

are asked to *"... take up the shield of faith, with which you can extinguish all the flaming arrows of the evil one."* This puts us on the victory side.

The practice of Christian unity is well illustrated by the following "One another" Scriptural statements given below:

- Love one another - John 13:34-35

- Mutually depend on one another - Romans 12:5

- Be devoted to one another - Romans 12:10

- Outdo one another in showing favour - Romans 12:10

- Rejoice with one another - Romans 12:15

- Have the same mind to one another - Romans 12:16

- Do not judge one another - Romans 14:13

- Build one another up - Romans 14:19

- Accept one another - Romans 15:7

- Counsel one another - Romans 15:14

- Wait for one another - 1 Corinthians 11:33

- Serve one another - Galatians 5:13

- Bear one another's burdens - Galatians 6:2

- Be kind to one another - Ephesians 4:32

- Forgive one another - Ephesians 4:32

- Forebear with one another - Colossians 3:13

- Admonish one another with all wisdom - Colossian 3:16

- Encourage one another - 1 Thessalonians 5:11

- Live in peace with one another - 1 Thessalonians 5:13

- Stir up one another - Hebrews 10:24

- Do not speak evil against one another - James 4:11

- Do not grumble against one another - James 5:9

- Confess your faults to one another - James 5:16

- Pray for one another - James 5:16

- Offer hospitality to one another - 1 Peter 4:9

- Fellowship with one another - 1 John 1:7

Fellowship

When we become Christians, we are brought into a common family relationship with God and other Christian believers, and this relationship is referred to as Christian fellowship. This gives us a common purpose as ordained by God. In this respect Christian fellowship is unique, as these special characteristics of friendship and purpose unite Christians throughout the world.

When we become Christians, God plants the desire in us to desire friendship with others and an ever-closer union with Himself. When we become Christians, we usually recognise the characteristics of other Christians, and this enables friendships to form relatively quickly between people who did not previously know one another.

We become part of the 'Body of Christ'– part of the collective body of those with a common relationship by faith in the Lord Jesus Christ.

For the Christian, fellowship with other like-minded believers is very important as it is a continuous source of strength, encouragement and practical help.

The Early Church:

> *"devoted themselves to the apostles' teaching and to the **fellowship**, to the breaking of bread and to prayer."*
>
> *(Acts 2:42 emphasis added)*

Thirsting for God

We live in a world where life for many is an unending rush to meet all the daily needs of work, home life and leisure. There are those at the other end of the spectrum whose life is a daily struggle for survival amidst natural disasters and poverty. However, whether we are wealthy or poor, in good or poor health, or whatever our circumstances or position in society, we all need to initially seek and find God for ourselves.

After we find God, there is always a need to know him better, to hear 'His voice' more clearly and to learn to follow His lead more closely. There is a basic human desire to seek after God, and this pursuit can occur in various ways. It can come out of a desperate need to hear God and make contact with Him, or out of a desire to know Him better.

The scriptures below relate to thirsting for God. They reveal something about the intent of the seeker(s) and their surrounding circumstances:

- Moses sought the favour of the Lord -

Exodus 32:11

- Those who seek God will find him -
Deuteronomy 4:29, Psalms 9:10

- Due to a famine, David sought the Lord 2
Samuel 21:1

- A repentant king sought the Lord's favour - 2
Kings 13:4

- When people humble themselves, and pray
and seek God's face, he hears and answers
them - 2 Chronicles 7:14

- The people sought God and he gave them
rest from their enemies - 2 Chronicles 14:7

- People in distress, sought and found God - 2
Chronicles 15:3-5, 20:3-7

- Whilst the king sought God, he gave him
success - 2 Chronicles 26:5

- When Hezekiah the king sought God and
worked wholeheartedly, he prospered - 2
Chronicles 31:20-21

- People separated themselves from unclean
practices in order to seek the Lord - Ezra
6:21

- David sought the Lord, he answered and brought him deliverance - Psalms 34:4, Psalms 143:5-9

- David's experience was that those who sought the Lord lacked nothing good - Psalms 34:10

- There is an urgency to seek the Lord while he may be found - Isaiah 55:6

- People will find God when they seek him with all their heart - Jeremiah 29:13

- People will find God when they firstly admit their guilt - Hosea 5:15

- There are times of famine of hearing the words of the Lord - Amos 8:11-13

- Happiness comes to those who thirst for righteousness - Matthew 5:6

- Those who seek will find - Matthew 7:7

- Those who believe in the Lord Jesus Christ will never be thirsty. - John 6:35, 7:37

- God waits for people to seek him, because he is near us - Acts 17:27

- God rewards those who earnestly seek Him - Hebrews 11:6

- To those who are thirsty for God, he will freely give the water of life - Revelation 21:6

In this pursuit we often spend most of our time and energy on issues such as Christian principles, doctrine and lifestyle. Whilst important, spending time getting to know God better is most important. David was a prime example of this. His closeness to God was reflected in his statement - *"My soul clings to you; your right hand upholds me."* (Psalms 63:8)

It is very important to know the characteristics that God is looking for in those who profess to follow Him. Some of those key characteristics of the persons he esteems are to be humble and contrite in spirit, and tremble at His word (Isaiah 66:2). In Psalm 63:1-6, we see David earnestly thirsting after God. From time to time we all experience a sense of dryness in our Christian life, and this can be caused through many factors such as mental, physical, emotional or spiritual exhaustion; sin; business pressures and the like. We need to recognise and confess this, and dedicate time to refocus on God, seek Him afresh and meditate on Him through his Word.

In Psalms 107:8-9 we see God meeting the need of those who are hungry and thirsty for Him, and how he heard, delivered and healed them.

The Presence of God

Whether as individuals or in a group, Christians can know something of 'the Presence of God' in an almost tangible way, and know within themselves that they are in a special place near to God. At this time, they sense the awe of the occasion and feel the acceptance and pleasure of this privileged position that brings in its wake consequences such as joy, confidence, peace and harmony. Many of the experiences referred to above can be seen in the Scriptures quoted below. The range of the Scriptures referred to that relate to this subject vary from a general sense of His Presence to that which is of a more intimate nature, and this should be borne in mind as the following Biblical references are considered.

- After Cain had killed his brother, we read, *"Cain went out from the Lord's presence"* (Genesis 4).

- A situation of harmony and sacrifices happened in the presence of God (Exodus 18:12)

- Moses was not prepared to lead the people on their journey towards the "Promised Land" unless he was assured of God's

Presence with them. (Exodus 33:14-19)

- When Moses came out from the presence of the Lord, his face was radiant, but he did not know it. (Exodus 34: 30-35)

- The Israelite leaders and people stood in the presence of the Lord to enter into a covenant with Him. (Deuteronomy 29:10-15)

- God revealed himself to Elijah when he was in his presence. (1 Kings 19:9-13)

- The Israelites forsook all the commands of the Lord, worshipped idols, practised divination and sorcery, so the Lord removed them from his presence. (2 Kings 17:16-20)

- The people praised the Lord, made sacrifices and feasted with great joy in the Lord's presence. (1 Chronicles 29:20-22)

- Jehoshaphat was confident of having prayers heard and answered in God's presence even when troubles come. (2 Chronicles 20:9)

- The king of Judah's prayer was heard when he humbled himself and repented in the Lord's presence. (2 Chronicles 34:27)

- Because of guilt, people could not stand in God's presence. (Ezra 9:15)

- The arrogant cannot stand in God's presence. (Psalms 5:5)

- God's presence provides a shelter to those who take refuge in Him (Psalms 31:19-20).

- God's presence is a gateway to spiritual restoration (Psalms 51:9-12).

- Those who speak falsely will not stand in God's presence (Psalms 101:7).

- Those who oppose God will one day tremble in His presence (Ezekial 38:20).

- The Lord Jesus Christ enjoyed the presence of God the Father (John 17:3-5).

- There is joy in God's presence (Acts 2:28).

- People hear from God when in His presence (Acts 10:32-33).

- Believers in the Lord Jesus Christ will spend eternity in His presence (2 Corinthians 4:13-14).

- Believers will be blameless and joyful in God's presence (1 Thessalonians 3:9-13).

- Those who do not know God will suffer eternally and be shut out from His presence (2 Thessalonians 1:8-9).

- God is able to keep His own people and present them in His glorious presence (Jude 1:24-25).

- Repentance precedes coming into His presence, (Isaiah 59:1-3.)

- King David, having sinned and repented, wanted to be reassured that he had not been cast out of God's presence, (Psalms 51:9-12).

We can come into a worship service, but still not enter His presence because there is a blockage in our personal relationship with God, due to the fact that there is sin in our lives that we have not confessed and repented of.

- We are each encouraged to seek God's face (1 Chronicles 16:10-11).

- His presence is known in the congregation -- see (2 Chronicles 5:11-14).

- When we are in God's presence and he 'speaks' to us who have a relationship with Him, that 'word' must be received with faith and acted on with grace and humility. For these 'words' are given for the common good of believers, for their strengthening, encouragement, comfort and edification. (1 Corinthians 12:7, 13:1-2, 14:1-4, 2 Peter 1:19-21).

- In Jonah 1:1-17 we see how Jonah, a man of God, intended to flee from the presence of the Lord because he did not want to do what God had asked him, and the subsequent problems he caused for himself and others. After God had disciplined him, he brought blessing to others through him. A lesson here is that we should seek to remain in His will, and so in His presence.

Praise and Worship

Our whole lives are meant to be an expression of worship, and hence 'praise' is a part of worship as it is part of life. Key parts of worship are expressed by time spent in adoration in His presence and living a lifestyle that reflects that of a devoted, loving disciple in every part of our lives, and so use all the time He has given us to reveal something of the nature and effect of our God to those around us. No part of our life is secular but it is all-spiritual and hence, all activities and attitudes will reflect our submission to, and our worship of, God.

Praise and worship are natural things that people do when they respond to a situation or action that takes place, and this is especially true when people form a relationship with the living God Jesus Christ. Prominent people one would expect to see praising and worshipping God would be those directly involved in the service of the church like pastors, vicars, church leaders and worship leaders. However, this would also include all the this does not exclude other people in the congregation, who often express their praise and worship in other ways, including practical work using a range of skills to further the aims of reaching out to meet the needs of people near and far. Some may work in a secular job and use some of their money to support the church or Christian organisations, whilst other Christians may work in a caring role as a nurse, doctor or as a worker in a care home. Many Christians see their role as a teacher caring for children to influence them by letting them see their character, whether they know, or not, that they are Christians.

Praise

In a time of praise, we have an opportunity to express our thanks to God in recognition of His attributes of character, his acts of love, grace and mercy. We can also acknowledge with gratitude His greatness, majesty, uniqueness and holiness, as

One who has all wisdom and knowledge and is absolute truth, always acts in purity, righteousness and all-knowing, just judgement. Also, we acknowledge Him as being God Almighty, the Creator of heaven and earth.

In 'praise' we lift His name above all others. Throughout the Bible there are a variety of ways in which praise is expressed and these include the voice in word, in singing and in shouting - and include physical expressions such as raising hands, clapping, kneeling, standing and laying prostrate. These should be the free expression of the individual believer at that time reflecting feelings varying from joy to earnest acknowledgements of sadness with tears of repentance.

Praise comes out of our worship, and its value directly relates to the quality and obedience of our worshipful lives. Praising God whilst remaining in an unforgiven state towards God or another person is just singing and is unacceptable to Him.

The Psalmist praised God not because He spares us pain and anguish, but because He is with us in them, for our growth and His glory (Psalm 41). There are many varied expressions of praise in the Bible as shown by the Scriptures given below:

- Psalms 43:3-4 states that we should praise God *"with joy and delight and with the harp."*

- Colossians 3:15-17 invites people to *"sing psalms, hymns and spiritual songs with gratitude in your hearts to God."*

In the Bible, a wide range of musical instruments were used, and therefore, in principle, a wide range of updated instruments can be used to-day as long as they serve the purpose of aiding sung expressions of praise to God.

Worship

It is an inbuilt characteristic in people that they desire someone or something to worship, to adore or pay homage to. This is borne out by history up to the present day, and is seen in the formation of many religions throughout the world. Even when a previously unknown tribe is found, the explorer discovers that they worship some type of god in the form of idols, sun, moon, trees, animals and the like.

One of the key reasons why this book has been written and compiled is to meet this basic need that people have in the most fulfilling way possible. This is done by pointing all people to the character of God as revealed in the Bible, and the whole approach to the subject starts through introducing them to this God. This approach provides the basis and reason for people to worship Him, appreciate what He has done for them and so come to believe in Him, know and love Him.

From this introduction to the subject, let us begin this most worthwhile of all quests by coming to appreciate, then to know and worship the unique living God of the Bible. People will then discover the true source and power of a new life, a life of assured hope, followed by eternal life.

Many biblical words relate to the giving of willing service to God. The giving of devotion and honour is demonstrated by walking upright before God in justice, love and humility (Micah 6:8).

Worship is also expressed by living in obedience and presenting ourselves to God, body, soul and spirit as a living sacrifice (Romans 12:1-2). In Genesis 22:1-18 it says that because Abraham obeyed God and was prepared to sacrifice his only son, God declared that he would make Abraham's descendants as numerous as the stars in the sky, and through them bless all nations on earth. From this story of Abraham, a lifestyle lived with faith in God and sacrificial giving coupled with obedience to God, is the attitude we should have in worship

The following Scripture reveals the attitude people should have in worship:

"Yet a time is coming and has now come

when the true worshippers will worship the Father in spirit and truth, for they are the kind of worshippers the Father seeks. God is spirit, and his worshippers must worship in spirit and in truth."

(John 4:23-24 also Hebrews 12:28-29)

Whilst worship can be a response to a personal relationship with God, it can also be expressed through a group of people, as in a congregation. Biblical scholars give the meaning of 'worship' in the New Testament Greek as – to do obeisance to, to prostrate oneself, to adore on one's knees. An example of 'bowing down' in worship is found in Job 1:20-22, and his action here shows complete submission to God, and as the whole story of Job shows that for a long period of time it cost him a great deal, but in the end, he was greatly blessed. The word 'worship' comes from the Anglo-Saxon word 'weothscipe' meaning to give worth to something. To-day the word 'worship' is generally taken to mean to give worth to something or someone. It has been said that *"worship that costs nothing is worth nothing"* (2 Samuel 24:24 and Mark 14:3-9). The quality of our service for God is a key expression of our worship, and this needs to be matched by our daily living for God for it to have value.

It is recommended that there should be an

acknowledgement of God at the outset of a worship service face by addressing him in worship and praise and then progress towards our response to Him. If this general approach is adopted, it is right to consider first His character, attributes and supernatural actions, as this gives us the substance on which to decide our response to Him.

Worship begins in the spiritual but also affects the physical, an example being that Jews rock back and forward when they pray. Postures in the Bible include lying face down, kneeling in His presence, standing with uplifted hands. Worship requires honest reality, truth and repentance in those who worship God.

In Nehemiah. 8:5-12 we observe that worship was preceded by reading the Word of God and blessing the Lord with the people lifting up their hands, and this led to the people bowing their heads and worshipping with their faces to the ground, followed by weeping due to confession of sin, and ending in joy. Also, in Nehemiah 9:1-3 it is interesting and challenging to note that the people fasted, repented, confessed their sin, read the Word of God, *then they worshipped – the worship came last.*

In view of the above Scriptures it might be a wise exercise for many churches to consider adopting a wider range of expression of, or types of declaration in, worship, in addition to singing. On a cautionary note, whilst a worship leader, worship group or choir may enhance the praise or worship of God, it can also become a substitute for it, and in such a case the congregation can be 'carried along' with the emotionalism of the situation. When this happens, we are in danger of our worship not being a true reflection of the condition of our hearts.

In Exodus. 20:25 and Joshua. 8:31 it refers to the fact that an altar should not be built from hewn stones, as man's workmanship on them would defile them. This could be a warning to us that we should not display *"man's workmanship"* in a worship service, e.g. any person(s), self-aggrandisement in any way, that could distract our attention away from Him whom we have come to worship.

When we truly worship God, we are submitting to His will, accepting the fact that His will is best. There are biblical Scriptures that give a prophetic warning to those who do not worship the God of the Bible, or recognise Him as the only true God. For example, we are told:

> *"It is written: 'As surely as I live,' says the Lord, 'Every knee will bow before me; every tongue will confess to God.'"*
> *(Romans 14:11-12; this refers to Isaiah 45:23-24)*

So then, each of us will give an account of himself to God'. Also, in Isaiah 45:24 it warns those who oppose God that they will be put to shame. [23]

Endnotes

1:   see Hebrews 5:11-14

2:   see Proverbs 4:23, Matthew 12:34, Psalm 51:10, Acts 20:24

3:   see Psalm 37:3-9, 46:1-3, Proverbs 3:5-8

4:   see John 3:16-18, Acts 16:29-34, Romans 3:21-24

5:   se also Acts 9:17, 1 Timothy 4:14; 1 Timothy 5:22, Hebrews 6:2

6:   see also 2 Timothy 1:5-7, Titus 1:5-9

7:   see Acts 14:23, 20:17, Philippians 1:1, 1 Timothy 5:17, Titus 1:5

8:   see Exodus 17:5-7, Numbers 20:6-12, Deuteronomy 3:23-27

9:   John 15:5; 1 Peter 4:10

10: see also Proverbs 22:4, Acts 20:18-19, Philippians 2:3

11: see also 1 Peter 5:1-3

12: see also Proverbs 27:19

13: see Romans 6:19-23

14: see Romans 3:22-23, Psalms 111:10, 1 Peter 1:13-16

15: see also Romans 13:1-5; Ephesians 5:21-24; James

4:6-7

16: see also Acts 10:19; 13:2; Romans 8:13-14; Galatians 5:18

17: see also John 18:15-17 & 25-27, Hebrews 4:11-13

18: see Matthew 20:25-28; Romans 12:4-5; 12:10, 1 Corinthians 16:15-16; Philippians 2:3-4; 1 Peter 5:5

19: see also: John 8:31-32; Colossians 1:22-23; Hebrews 3:14

20: see also see 1 Corinthians 12:4-7, & 14-20

21: see also see Ephesians 4:11-13, Philippians 1:27

22: see 1 Corinthians 1:9, 2 Corinthians 13:14, Philippians 2:1, 1 John 1:3

23: see also: Isaiah 66:23, Philippians 2:10-11

Chapter 5

Concluding Essential Thoughts

The Ultimate Aim

It is the sincere desire of the author that this book will have achieved its purpose of bringing new spiritual life, encouragement and enlightenment with biblical truth to the non-Christian, the seeker after truth, and the Christian alike. Also, in this pursuit for truth the author hopes that readers have come to appreciate that the Bible is the unique source for revealing God's wisdom, love, grace, forgiveness and direction for life, and the sure hope of eternal life that is offered to all people.

For those of another Faith, no faith, or those who are unclear about these matters, the author also hopes that the reader will find all the help they need in this book to experience the reality of a living, loving relationship with God.

The author has sought to provide solid, reliable evidence that can be found in that Faith - evidence of a Living God who communicates with people, answers prayers, makes positive changes to the character of people's lives, and as this evidence is provided in Christianity, then it is wise to compare it to what can be found in other Faiths. If, however, you have not accepted the Christian Faith because you're not convinced about the evidence, the importance, or the relevance of the issues presented, or you're fearful about the consequences of making that step into the Christian Faith, then please consider the destiny that we all are travelling towards, as outlined below.

The Ultimate Destiny

Here are the steps of a typical life's journey in which a person:

Is born into a set of circumstances over which we have neither choice or control;

Has a family or no family upbringing, with or without love;

What Then?

Has none, some or much schooling;

Hears, or does not hear, about a religious Faith;

Accepts or rejects the Christian Faith;

Achieves none or some skills or qualifications;

Tries or gets desired job/money/place to live;

Tries or gets desired personal relationship;

Enjoys a good or not so good life;

Has health problems or an accident;

Thinks about what will happen at death;

Thinks about destiny, could it be Heaven or Hell?

Considers what determines their destiny?

Through some, or all, of these stages of life, we become aware that God is speaking to us in various ways. This is because He loves us and longs for us to enjoy the *best life*, and to achieve this, He has gradually been trying to help us to understand that it is only through repentance and trusting in the Lord Jesus Christ that we can find forgiveness and assurance that leads to the *best* destiny of heaven. Let us remember that God's heart has been revealed to us through the Bible when it affirms:

"God wants all men to be saved and to come
to a knowledge of the truth."

(1 Timothy 2:4)

Back Matter

Content Index

Subject Index